Lincoln on God and Country

By
Gordon Leidner

Introduction by
Michael Burlingame

WHITE MANE BOOKS

Copyright © 2000 by Gordon Leidner

ALL RIGHTS RESERVED—No part of this book may be reproduced in any form without permission in writing from the publisher, except by a reviewer who wishes to quote brief
passages in connection with a review.

This White Mane Books publication
was printed by
Beidel Printing House, Inc.
63 West Burd Street
Shippensburg, PA 17257-0152 USA

In respect for the scholarship contained herein, the acid-free paper used in this book
meets the guidelines for permanence and durability of the Committee on Production Guidelines for Book Longevity of the Council on Library Resources.

For a complete list of available publications
please write
White Mane Books
Division of White Mane Publishing Company, Inc.
P.O. Box 152
Shippensburg, PA 17257-0152 USA

Library of Congress Cataloging-in-Publication Data

Leidner, Gordon, 1954-
    Lincoln on God and country / by Gordon Leidner ; introduction by Michael Burlingame.
        p. cm.
    Includes bibliographical references and index.
    ISBN 1-57249-207-4 (alk. paper)
    1. Lincoln, Abraham, 1809-1865--Quotations. 2. Presidents--United
States--Quotations. 3. United States--Politics and government--Quotations, maxims, etc.
4. Conduct of life--Quotations, maxims, etc. I. Title.

E457.99 .L35 2000
973.7'092--dc21

                                                                      00-040831

PRINTED IN THE UNITED STATES OF AMERICA

To Michael, Jason, and Daniel—with a reminder that great men seek God.

Contents

Preface

The Declaration of Independence and the Constitution of the United States are today displayed harmoniously—one above the other—in the National Archives in Washington, D.C. Even though we think of them as the twin pillars and foundation of freedom, equality, and democracy, we sometimes forget that until the Thirteenth Amendment significantly changed the Constitution, the two documents were far from being equal themselves.

The Declaration of Independence stated a proposition: all men are created equal. At that time it was much more hope than fact, because when it was written, few men were actually "equal." Social status, wealth, religious beliefs, and—most obvious of all—race, exemplified the stratified nature of American society. This hierarchy was not as pronounced as it was in most European societies, but it was still there.

Nevertheless, the Declaration proposed that all men should be equal. Unfortunately, when less than a dozen years later some of those same men who authored it met with others to write the US Constitution, they assembled a governing document that ignored the earlier proposal. That the Constitution ignored the proposition all men are created equal and allowed slavery was neither accident nor oversight on the part of its writers. The right to continue to own slaves was adamantly supported by some of them, bitterly opposed by others, and reluctantly agreed to by most. Ashamed of their deviation from the proposal that all men are created equal, they never mentioned the word "slavery" in the text of the Constitution. References to it were made indirectly and hidden by euphemisms, but the message was nevertheless plain: all men were not created equal.

Abraham Lincoln, born in the slave state of Kentucky 21 years after the Constitution was adopted, struggled with the disparity between those two documents for most of his adult life. He had been taught to respect both of them as equal elements of democratic government. Lincoln stated that he "loved the sentiments of those old time men" who

wrote the Declaration of Independence, but as he grew older, he realized that those sentiments were confused. Thomas Jefferson and the co-
authors of the Declaration had argued eloquently for a system of
government that gave the poor man the same vote it gave the wealthy.
But George Washington and the signers of the Constitution later gave
the white man the right to enslave the black man.

Lincoln said, "If the Negro is a man, why then my ancient faith teaches
me that 'all men are created equal,' and that there can be no moral right in
connection with one man's making a slave of another."[1] As this book will
demonstrate, this statement represented a fundamental struggle in his life.

Although Lincoln's heart was with the Declaration on the issue of
equality, he was forced to accept the Constitution as law. As a lawyer, his
life's work was centered around interpretation and compliance with the
law. But when his heart and mind were in conflict, heart almost always
won out over mind. He may have pleaded for "cold, calculating reason" to
take precedence and for law of the land to become the political "religion"
of America, but in his life are many examples of where he placed mercy
before law. Among these are his many presidential pardons of soldiers
sentenced to death.

In successfully leading the war effort, Lincoln became the leader that
finally forced the nation to reconcile the Declaration of Independence and
the Constitution. Starting with a war to save the Union, he ended with a
war that not only saved the Constitution, but also fulfilled—or at least *began* to fulfill—the proposal expressed in The Declaration of Independence.
The Thirteenth Amendment, which abolished slavery, was passed largely
as a result of Lincoln's leadership.

Lincoln's religious beliefs are among the more controversial aspects
of our 16th president. Statements from his contemporaries seem to justify the reason he has been called everything from a prophet to an infidel.
His wife once said that her husband "was not a technical Christian,"[2] but
she also said he was a "religious man by nature."[3] In 1865, Lincoln's junior law partner, William Herndon, said that his senior partner was never
an orthodox Christian.[4] But then, 20 years later, Herndon seemed to have
doubts about his earlier statement.[5] Considering this, I have decided to
let Lincoln's words speak for themselves in regard to his religious beliefs, rather than relying on the interpretations of the people that knew
him.

This book is divided into two parts. Part I is a short biography of
Lincoln. Part II provides Lincoln's speeches and writings organized according to eight topics, i.e., Our Debt to the Nation's Founders, The People,
Government and Economy, Law and Politics, Freedom, Presidential Leadership, Faith in God, and Our Debt to Our Children. To place the Lincoln
quotes in context, I provide brief editorial comment and introduction for
each of them. Since this book is intended to be primarily a book of Lincoln

quotations, rather than interpretation, I have tried to limit my personal reflections to the Preface, Afterword, and an introductory paragraph for each chapter of Part II.

Introduction

One of the greatest of all Lincoln biographers, Benjamin P. Thomas, aptly observed that "Lincoln's style was peculiarly and distinctively his own, as distinctively his own as his unique personality. And by reason of its simplicity, frankness and utter lack of restraint it reflects his personality to a remarkable degree—to such a degree, in fact, that while we can learn much about Lincoln by reading what has been written of him by others, we cannot claim really to know him until we have read what he himself wrote and said."[1] In this volume, Gordon Leidner has judiciously selected revealing and characteristic utterances of Lincoln that illuminate the 16th president's character, values, and ideology.

Although Lincoln achieved his greatest eloquence in his forties and fifties, he showed signs even in his early adulthood of the spark of individuality that would characterize his later utterances. While canvassing for the state legislature at the age of 27, as one of his fellow Whig candidates for the General Assembly (Robert L. Wilson) recalled, Lincoln "took a leading part, espousing the Whig side of all those questions, manifesting Skill and tact in offensive and defensive debates, presenting his arguments with great force and ability, and boldly attacking the questions and positions taken by opposing Candidates." Wilson ascribed Lincoln's success as a debater to his unusual approach: "He was, on the stump, and in the Halls of Legislation a ready Debater, manifesting extraordinary ability in his peculiar manner of presenting his subject. He did not follow the beaten track of other Speakers, and Thinkers, but appeared to comprehend the whole situation of the Subject, and take hold of its first principles; He had a remarkable faculty for concentration, enabling him to present his subject in such a manner as nothing but conclusions were presented. He did not follow a system of ratiocination deducing conclusions from premises, laid down, and eliminated; but his mode of reasoning was purely analytical; his reasons and conclusions were always drawn from analogy. His memory was a great Store house in which was Stored away all the facts acquired by reading but principally by observation; and intercourse with men Woman and children, in their Social, and business relations; learning and weighing the motives that prompt each act in life. Supplying him with an inexhaustible fund of facts, from which he would draw conclusions, and illustrating every Subject however complicated with annecdotes drawn from all classes of Society, accomplishing the double purpose, of not only proving his Subject by the annecdote, But the annecdote itself possessing so much point and force, that no one ever forgets, after hearing Mr. Lincoln tell a Story, either the argument of the Story, the Story itself, or the author."[2]

One of Lincoln's stiffest political opponents in central Illinois, John Hill, offered a similar analysis of his remarkable eloquence.[3] "The convincing power of Mr. Lincoln's plain conversational method of address," recalled Hill, was "marvelous and almost iresistable, Plain, candid and honest, without the slightest effort at display or oratory." He carried his auditors "along to unconscious conviction. The benign expression of his face and his earnest interest in the subject, asserted with such simplicity, secured sympathetic absorption. All listened in close attention to the end, and when he had finished there pervaded a momentary solemn silence before his audience realised that it was the end."[4] Hill described Lincoln as "the planest man I ever heard." He "was not a speaker but a talker." Such was his "honesty, candor, and fairness" that it "was scarcely possible for an auditor not to believe every word uttered. The same in conversation. He left behind him on all occasions, a feeling one can not express of respect and that accompanied by affection for a good man."[5] Albert Taylor Bledsoe, who practiced law with Lincoln in the 1840s and collaborated with him as a leader of the Illinois Whig party, said that in Lincoln's speeches "there is, not infrequently, a homely strength, and a rustic beauty of expression, which are more effective than the oratorical periods of an [Edward] Everett or a [George] Bancroft. His simple, terse, plain, direct English, goes right home to the point."[6]

But as a young man, Lincoln could also be bombastic. With some justice, Bledsoe noted that Lincoln's first major address, a talk given to the Springfield Young Men's Lyceum when the speaker was 28, showed that sometimes Lincoln was "woefully given to *sesquipedalian* words, or, in Western phrase, *highfalutin* bombast." Referring to a few particularly banal observations, Bledsoe added: "To those familiar with his sober and pure style at a later age, these sophomoric passages will seem incredible."[7]

Lincoln changed dramatically in midlife.[8] At the age of 40, he was, as Benjamin P. Thomas put it, "an honest, capable, but essentially self-centered small-town politician of self-developed but largely unsuspected talents" and "a lucid thinker and a clever man before a crowd." Five years later he had become a different man, a "political analyst and debater of surpassing power," speaking "with a new seriousness, a new explicitness, a new authority," and thus he grew into "a statesman." The years from

1849 to 1854 were "among the most fruitful of his life," for "as he put aside all thought of political advancement and devoted himself to personal improvement, he grew tremendously in mind and character."[9]

Lincoln's first truly great address, delivered in 1854 at Peoria, Illinois, was, as Albert J. Beveridge noted, "wholly unlike any before made by him. Indeed, if it and his public utterances thereafter were placed side by side with his previous [pre-1854] speeches, and the authorship of them all were unknown, it would appear impossible that they had been written by the same man."[10]

The speeches and letters gathered here offer a revealing portrait of Lincoln in both phases of his remarkable career. We hear the purple prose, the satirical wit, and the occasional demagoguery of the 1830s and 1840s and the surpassing eloquence of the 1850s and 1860s. Masterpieces like the 1860 Cooper Union speech, the 1861 farewell address to Springfield, the 1863 Gettysburg address, and the 1865 second inaugural help make understandable Leo Tolstoy's assessment of Lincoln: "He was what Beethoven was in music, Dante in poetry, Raphael in painting, and Christ in the philosophy of life."[11]

MICHAEL BURLINGAME

Connecticut College
January 2000

Part I

Biography

Chapter 1
Lincoln's Life

Youth

Fifteen-year-old Abe Lincoln picked up the Bible and walked over to the old tree stump that would serve as his pulpit for the next half hour. The rest of the children, most of whom were younger, quickly took their places on the ground in front of the young preacher. He stood behind the stump, which like everything else was too short for him, and called out a greeting in imitation of one of the traveling evangelists they had recently heard at the Little Pigeon Creek Baptist Church.

Abe read aloud from the book of Psalms and then called for the first hymn. The congregation responded by singing out, "How tedious and tasteless the hours, when Jesus I no longer see . . ." and continued with the familiar John Newton hymn, without need of a hymnbook or prompting. Once the hymn was over, he began to preach. He repeated nearly word-for-word the sermon they had heard the day before. He walked back and forth in front of the congregation, imitating the mannerisms of the evangelist. As he preached, the children would cry out responses to his queries, and shout a hardy "Amen!" when appropriate. Finally he called for the last hymn, "Oh to Grace How Great a Debtor!" and closed with prayer.[1]

Abraham Lincoln was born on February 12, 1809, on a farm in Hardin County, Kentucky.[2] Soon after his birth, Abe's 10-year old cousin, Dennis Hanks, walked over to the Lincoln cabin to see the newborn. After Dennis held him for a while, the baby started to cry and grew red-faced, in spite of Dennis' efforts to quiet him. Finally he handed him back to his aunt and said disgustedly, "Take him, he'll never come to much."[3]

Abe's parents, typical of poor white farmers of western Kentucky, owned a farm that had been registered by a land title of dubious origin. Thomas and Nancy Lincoln's home, near Hodgenville, was known as the Sinking Spring Farm. Within three years of settling there, the defective land title made it necessary for them to leave. They moved to what would become

3

known as the Knob Creek place, about ten miles northeast of Sinking Spring. They lived at Knob Creek until Abe was about seven years old, and while there he briefly attended school with his older sister, Sarah.

Thomas and Nancy Lincoln were members of the Little Mount Separate Baptist Church in Kentucky. The Separate Baptists were different from other Baptists in that they accepted no creed except the Bible itself, and were staunchly antislavery. Their beliefs obviously had a lasting impact on him, as the adult Lincoln remained antislavery and insisted that he didn't want to join any church that confessed any creed other than Jesus' admonition to "love the Lord thy God with all thy heart and with all thy soul," and "thy neighbor as thyself."[4]

Land title problems caused them to move again—this time to Indiana—in December 1816. They packed up their essential family possessions such as the tools, spinning wheel, and cooking utensils, then traveled westward across the Ohio River. Traveling through the Indiana wilderness to their selected homesite on Little Pigeon Creek in Perry County,[5] Thomas Lincoln had to "cut his way to his farm with an ax, felling trees as he went."[6]

Their first winter in Indiana was harsh, and the Lincolns struggled to survive on wild game. They spent their evenings in a manner typical of the American pioneer families, storytelling, reading the Bible, and helping the children with their lessons. Abe and his sister used *Dilworth's Spelling Book* for both spelling and grammar lessons. This book, like so many schoolbooks of that day, consisted of many moral anecdotes, largely drawn from Proverbs and Psalms.[7]

Lincoln's mother, who was described by those that knew her as a kind and intelligent woman, narrated Bible stories to her children long before they were able to read. Lincoln's father, from whom Abe probably inherited his delight in storytelling, told his children about many of their ancestors' encounters with Indians, including how their grandfather Abraham had been killed by them in 1786.

In the fall of 1818, Nancy Lincoln contracted a fatal disease known as "the milk sick." When she was dying, she called her two children to her bedside to say goodbye. She asked them to be good and kind to their father, one another, and the world. She also expressed hope that they would revere and worship God as she had taught them.[8] She died soon after this.

Thomas Lincoln built a crude coffin and, with the help of Abe and Sarah, buried his wife in a clearing near their cabin. Thomas spent the next several months trying to be both provider and nurturer to his heart-broken children. Within a year he made a brief trip to Kentucky, married a widow, Sarah Bush Johnston, and brought her and her three children back to Indiana with him. Sarah Lincoln became an affectionate mother to Abe and his sister, doing her best to treat them the same as her own children.

In Indiana the Lincolns joined the Little Pigeon Creek Baptist Church. This church was probably of the type known as "hard-shell" Baptist, whose members had strong Calvinist leanings and believed that only those pre-destined by God would be saved. The Lincoln family life revolved around the church, and they attended regularly. Thomas helped plan and build the Little Pigeon Creek meeting house, and served as a sort of deacon or elder.

Abe witnessed a great deal of hardship while growing up, because disease took many lives in the rural community. It was said that Thomas Lincoln, who was a carpenter by trade, "was always making a coffin for someone." Abe had a younger brother that had died in infancy, and it seemed that nearly every home lost at least one child. The settlers accepted these trials and carried on, showing a remarkable resiliency and optimism. For most, including the Lincolns, their faith helped them endure their losses. They believed that the hardships were somehow a part of the Almighty's judicious plan, trusted that He knew what was best, and believed He would call for everyone at their appointed time. The belief that the deceased had gone to heaven and would one day be seen again gave survivors comfort and the courage to carry on.

Although Abe witnessed tragedies, he also saw many successes. He watched his father and neighbors establish, with hard work and determi-nation, the Little Pigeon Creek community in the middle of the wilderness. In 1820 nine families, including almost 50 children, lived within a one-mile radius of the Lincoln cabin. As the community became more established, the people constructed a church, a school, and other community buildings. They cleared fields, split rails, and put up fences. All this was done using free labor, as opposed to slave—a fact that was not lost on either Thomas Lincoln or his son.

In Indiana, Abe and his sister attended school for a few months. He was a natural scholar, and eagerly read books such as *Robinson Crusoe, Aesop's Fables*, and *Pilgrim's Progress*. Abe's formal education was sporadic, and would eventually amount to less than a year in public school. Virtu-ally all of what he learned was by the method known today as homeschooling.

Lincoln was raised in an era when the Bible was central in the lives of most Americans. For most families, Abe's included, it was probably the only book they owned.[9] It is noteworthy that the small amount of public education Abe received included Bible reading as an essential element of the curriculum. By the time he was a young man he had memorized a great deal of the Bible, including the 23rd Psalm and part of the fourteenth chap-ter of John.

When he grew older, Abe's father frequently took advantage of his son's physical strength and stature. He used him to not only work his own farm, but would frequently hire his teenage son out to other farmers and use the money Abe earned for the benefit of the family.

As Abe grew older, he became increasingly dissatisfied with the physical labor involved in farming. Unlike most farmers' sons, he did not develop a love for hunting, tending livestock, or raising crops. He delighted in books and storytelling. He would listen attentively to adult conversations, and after the visitors departed would barrage his parents with questions. He would repeat to himself what the grownups had said, trying to comprehend the meaning of every word, and it angered him when adults talked to him in a manner he couldn't understand.

When Abe was 17, his 19-year-old sister, Sarah, married a neighbor, Aaron Grigsby. Tragically, Sarah died giving birth to her first child in January 1828. Abe took it very hard, and wept bitterly. He always believed that Sarah and her baby might have lived if a doctor had been summoned in time.

In December 1828, at the age of 19, Abe was given the opportunity to help a man take a flatboat of goods to New Orleans. James Gentry, owner of a local general store, hired him for $8 per month, plus passage back by steamboat. This trip was one of the most exciting events of his life, and it gave Abe a hunger to see more of the world beyond the wilderness.

When Abe was nearly 21, his father decided to move the family from Indiana to Illinois. The Lincoln family loaded their possessions onto ox-drawn wagons and headed westward. The journey was made during the winter months, and Abe had to walk alongside the wagons and guide the oxen on frozen roads. At a river crossing, when his dog jumped from a wagon and broke through the ice, he rescued him from drowning. "I could not bear to lose my dog," he recalled years later.[10]

Abe and his family settled near Decatur, Illinois. He helped build a log cabin and put in the first crop, then left his parents to set out on his own.

Young Legislator

Lincoln stood before the small crowd in Pappsville, Illinois, anxiously waiting for his turn to speak. Even at the age of twenty-three he had not outgrown his gangling appearance. His hands were too big, his Adam's apple too pronounced, and his pants too short. His height seemed ludicrous when compared to the men around him. But in spite of these distractions, there was an earnest expression on his face, and he silently re-read the speech he had prepared for this occasion—his first announcement of candidacy for political office.

When about to begin his speech, Lincoln was interrupted by a fight that broke out in the crowd. He recognized that his friend Rowan Herndon was in trouble, so he stopped what he was doing and pushed his way through the audience. Joining his friend, he quickly ended the fight by grabbing one of Herndon's opponents by the shirt collar and seat of his pants and throwing him twelve feet through the air.

Lincoln returned to the front of the crowd, who suddenly quieted down and took a more avid interest in what this tall young man was doing. He said, "Fellow Citizens, I presume you all know who I am—I am humble Abraham Lincoln. I have been solicited by many friends to become a candidate for the Legislature. My politics are short and sweet, like the old woman's dance. I am in favor of a national bank. I am in favor of the internal improvement system and a high protective tariff. These are my sentiments and political principles. If elected I shall be thankful; if not it will be all the same."[11]

Lincoln arrived in New Salem, Illinois, during the summer of 1831, at the age of 22. The village consisted of about 15 or 20 cabins, located along the banks of the Sangamon River in the central part of the state. People welcomed the affable Lincoln, and a businessman by the name of Denton Offut asked him to help build and manage a general store. After helping Offut cut the logs, construct the store, and stock it with general merchandise, Lincoln settled down to his job of selling goods.

Although he didn't sell much in the way of merchandise, Lincoln quickly made a lot of friends. He swapped stories, told jokes, and did small favors for people. As a store clerk he developed a reputation for honesty and was soon being asked to act as a judge or arbiter in various contests, races, and arguments. One resident later claimed that "Mr. Lincoln's judgment was final in all that region of the country. People relied implicitly upon his honesty, integrity, and impartiality."[12]

His physical stature, strength, and athletic ability made him very popular with the toughs of the small town. He demonstrated his physical prowess by wrestling a local bully, Jack Armstrong. Doing well in this contest, he won the respect of Armstrong and his friends, who were known as the Clary's Grove Boys. In them Lincoln developed an army of allies, and at future campaign rallies he rarely had to worry about hecklers in the audience.

Lincoln continued his self-education by studying subjects such as geometry, literature, and Shakespeare. He became a friend of the local teacher, Mentor Graham, who helped him tackle previously neglected subjects such as grammar and speech. It became a common sight in New Salem to see Lincoln reading or walking around with a book tucked under his arm.

The Offut store failed less than a year after it was opened, and Lincoln surprised everyone when he announced he would run for the state legislature. His campaign was interrupted fairly quickly, however, when Chief Black Hawk and about five hundred Sauk and Fox Indian warriors entered Illinois, seeking to recover land that had been taken from them.

He postponed the political campaign and joined a militia unit to fight Black Hawk. With the exception of the fact Lincoln was elected captain by the men, very little came out of this experience. The soldiers Lincoln was with spent weeks in a vain attempt to find Black Hawk, and never even got a glimpse of the enemy until an old drunken Indian stumbled into their camp. Finally, other militia units forced Black Hawk to surrender, and Lincoln returned to his political campaign.

In this, his first campaign, Lincoln demonstrated fledgling political savvy when he announced his platform. He was in favor of various public improvements, and carefully avoided controversial national issues. He supported internal improvements such as better roads, new canals, improvements to the Sangamon River, and construction of a railroad. He believed everyone should be provided at least a moderate education so that they could "read the Scriptures and other works."[13]

Although the young Whig candidate won overwhelmingly in his own precinct, collecting 277 out of 300 votes, he was defeated because he was unknown in other precincts. He would later say that this was the only time he was ever defeated in a political contest by the "direct vote" of the people.

After losing the election, Lincoln went into partnership with village resident William Berry and opened another general store in New Salem. Again Lincoln worked faithfully behind the counter, selling goods, telling stories and swapping jokes, but Berry drank up all the profits. This store failed too, and when Berry died a couple of years after the start of the partnership, Lincoln was left with a debt of $1,100. This sum, which he referred to as the "national debt," would take him 15 years to pay off.

One of the more serious subjects Lincoln talked about while sitting around the Berry store was religion. Although there are today no writings by Lincoln that reflect disrespect for the Christian faith, there are some accounts by residents of New Salem that indicate he frequently debated the historical accuracy of the Bible. Lincoln would later say that he developed a temporary belief in what he called the "Doctrine of Necessity." This, according to author Elton Trueblood, was what was also called "determinism," and is not far removed from the doctrine of predestination Lincoln learned during his childhood at the Little Pigeon Creek Baptist Church.[14]

After the Berry store failed, Lincoln's friends helped him secure an appointment as postmaster of New Salem in May 1833. That modest income helped, but it proved insufficient to cover his bills, so he taught himself surveying. He soon became deputy surveyor and began working in New Salem and surrounding communities.

Still not completely satisfied with his life in New Salem, Lincoln borrowed books and studied law. He read *Blackstone's Commentaries* and the *Revised Laws of Illinois*, and soon began pleading minor cases before the local justice of the peace, Bowling Green. Under the tutelage of Green, Lincoln improved his speaking skills and knowledge of the law.

Not deterred by his previous failure in politics, Lincoln ran for the state legislature again in 1834. This time he secured the support of both the

Whig and Democratic parties, and apparently made no announcement of a formal political platform. He was successful, and on December 1 he went to the state capital, Vandalia, to take his seat as a representative from Sangamon County.

In his first term in the state legislature, Lincoln had an advantage over other new legislators because he shared a room with fellow Whig and minority leader John T. Stuart. He learned much from Stuart in the way of the practical functioning of state government. Stuart taught him how to write bills, introduce them, and maneuver them through the legislature. Although Lincoln did not make any speeches in his first term, he was appointed to a dozen special committees. He also demonstrated a great deal of independent thinking, because even though he was a freshman legislator, he was not averse to voting against the Whig Party on issues of conscience.

In 1836 Lincoln ran for re-election to the legislature, and a surviving campaign speech reveals a much more confident, savvy campaigner. During this run for office Lincoln was forced to deal with his political opponents' efforts to discredit him in a "whispering" campaign. An Illinois democrat, Robert Allen, came through Springfield claiming that he knew "something" about Lincoln that, if public knowledge, would cause people to refuse to vote for him. Hearing of this, Lincoln decided to take advantage of his reputation for honesty, and ordered Allen to "make public" any secrets he knew. Allen quickly dropped the issue, and Lincoln won the election.

In Lincoln's second term, with the arrival of 66 freshman legislators, he stepped up to senior status. He also became one of the "Long Nine," a group of nine politicians from Sangamon County that were each more than six feet tall. This group included seven members of the House and two state senators, all of whom were Whigs, or at least leaned towards Whig policy. They became an extremely influential force in the legislature.

In the 1836 session of the Illinois Legislature, Lincoln met the man that would become his long time political nemesis, Stephen A. Douglas. Douglas, a Democrat from Jacksonville, Illinois, was a skilled lawyer and speaker that would soon develop a national reputation in politics. Rather than staying in the state legislature like Lincoln, he quickly moved on to the Illinois Supreme Court, US Congress, and US Senate.

Lincoln was instrumental in passing two significant bills during his second term. The first one, an internal improvements bill, proved disastrous to the state's financial stability for several decades. As a member of the Finance Committee, Lincoln and the bi-partisan committee attempted to fund a huge improvements program with bond issues. They borrowed more than 10 million dollars in order to begin what proved to be an extensive, poorly planned program to construct railroads, roads, bridges, and canals all over the state. Instead of concentrating on a few strategic lanes of transportation, they built bridges and roads in a haphazard manner, evidently hoping that towns would spring up as a result.

This ruined the state economically, because very few of the projects bore fruit. Within a couple of years, the interest on the debt became a significant burden on the state's resources, and it would finally take 45 years to completely pay off. Although each party would later try to blame the other for the debt, both Whigs and Democrats were at fault.

Another significant bill Lincoln helped pass was the relocation of the state capital from Vandalia to Springfield. Both Lincoln and the Long Nine were instrumental in its passage. Although it was later claimed that Lincoln used plums from the internal improvements funds to buy votes for the move to Springfield, subsequent research has disproved this.[15]

Lincoln was accepted as John T. Stuart's law partner when he was admitted to the Sangamon Bar at the close of the 1836 session. This was fortunate for Lincoln, because Stuart ran one of the most successful law practices in Springfield. Now that he was a practicing attorney, Lincoln decided to leave New Salem and take up residence in Springfield. He moved in with a merchant by the name of Joshua Speed in March of 1837.

Lincoln again won re-election, and when he returned for his third term in 1838, he acquired a stronger leadership role because John T. Stuart had left for a seat in Congress. Although Lincoln lost a bid for Speaker of the House, he became the de facto floor leader for the Whigs. In this term, a great deal of his efforts in the Finance Committee involved the defense of the State Bank against attacks by the Democrats. He also worked hard to resolve debt issues emerging because of the internal improvements bill.

In 1839, he met his future wife, Mary Todd. Mary was a well-educated young lady from a prominent Kentucky family, and had recently moved to Springfield to live with her sister and brother-in-law, Elizabeth and Ninian Edwards. The Edwards home had become a sort of a social center in Springfield and was frequented by most of the town's young bachelors, including Lincoln.

Mary Todd was politically astute, and made no secret of her desire to marry the man that would "one day be president." Although she had an interest in many of the men, including Stephen A. Douglas, she soon fell in love with the tallest and homeliest of the lot, Lincoln. In 1840, during Lincoln's fourth and last term in the state legislature, he and Mary became romantically involved, perhaps even engaged.[16]

Lincoln's fourth term was in Springfield, instead of Vandalia, and the new state capitol building was nearly finished when the first session started. By this time, Lincoln had become one of the Illinois Whig Party's most influential members. In the presidential campaign of that year, the Whigs ran William Henry Harrison against the Democrats' candidate, Martin Van Buren. Lincoln became an active campaigner for Harrison, and in the course of doing so engaged Stephen A. Douglas in both formal and informal debates. During one debate, Lincoln used a letter obtained from Van Buren to prove that Douglas was making misleading statements about a campaign biography of the Democratic presidential candidate. This so enraged Douglas that he took the book and threw it into the audience.[17]

In Lincoln's fourth term he suffered with poor health and a waning interest in the affairs of the state legislature. Lincoln had a melancholy personality, but these problems may have resulted primarily from his erratic romance with Mary. In early January 1841, Lincoln broke off their relationship, and he subsequently went through a long bout of depression that adversely impacted his effectiveness as legislator. His leadership was sadly missed by the Whigs, especially during a fight with the Democrats in the latter's effort to increase the number of state Supreme Court justices from four to nine. The Democrats succeeded, and shifted the balance of power by adding five new Democrats, including Stephen A. Douglas, to the state's supreme court.

Lincoln wrote several letters to his old friend Joshua Speed, seeking his advice about women. In a letter to Speed in 1842, Lincoln stated his belief that God had "made me (Lincoln) one of the instruments" to bring Speed and his fiancée together, and was trusting the Lord to do the same for him, too.[18]

Although they avoided each other for many months, Lincoln and Mary began seeing each other again in late summer of 1842. They secretly undertook a political project—writing a series of anonymous letters for the *Sangamon Journal*, lampooning a local Democratic politician, James Shields. This resulted in Lincoln's being challenged to a duel by Shields and, more importantly, the return of a romance between Lincoln and Mary.

Even though Lincoln had once said in jest he could "never be satisfied with anyone block-head enough to have me,"[19] he and Mary were married on November 4, 1842. Their first son, Robert Todd, was born less than a year later. After marrying, Lincoln occasionally attended church in Springfield with his wife, but remained true to his pledge that he would not join any church that had more than Jesus' first commandment as its creed and did not join.

Lincoln, remembering he had once said, "whatever woman should cast her lot with mine . . . it is my intention to do all in my power to make her happy and contented," took his marriage seriously. But Mary, who came from a wealthy family and was accustomed to having her own way, was difficult for Lincoln to please. When they were first married they lived in a two-room apartment at the Globe Tavern, and it became obvious to Lincoln that he would have to provide a better home for his family. Consequently, he worked hard at expanding his law practice, and was soon able to purchase a modest house in Springfield.

Earliest known photograph of Lincoln, taken probably in 1846 at the age of 37.

Library of Congress

Earliest known photograph of Mary Lincoln, probably taken in 1846 when she was 28 years old.

Library of Congress

Midlife

On July 27, 1848, 39-year old Congressman Abraham Lincoln stood before the US House of Representatives. The Democratic Party's presidential candidate, Lewis Cass, was about to become the victim of the freshman congressman's well-known political sarcasm. Lincoln addressed the Speaker of the House in a respectful, familiar tone, and asked him if he realized that he had once been a military hero. His reason for this question was to draw a parallel between his obviously minor accomplishments as a captain of militia in the Black Hawk War and the similarly minor— although much trumpeted—accomplishments of "General" Cass in the War of 1812.

Lincoln proceeded to lampoon Cass expertly, comparing the latter's broken sword to his own "bent musket." He stated that although Cass undoubtedly was better at picking huckleberries, Lincoln probably surpassed him in charges on the wild onions. He implied the general had probably never seen any actual fighting, and expressed hope that Lincoln's friends would not make fun of HIM, by trying to claim he was a military hero, in the way Cass's friends had made fun of their candidate.

Lincoln's law partnership with John T. Stuart continued until its amicable dissolution in April 1841. Lincoln was then accepted as junior partner by one of the most renowned lawyers of the state, Stephen T. Logan. Logan, a small man of dour countenance, was a stickler for precise documentation and thorough trial preparation. These qualities had a positive impact on Lincoln, who had become rather haphazard in his legal methods during his previous partner's absence at Congress.

But what Lincoln lacked in systematic preparation he made up in power of persuasion with juries. Lincoln had a natural rapport with juries, and made use of humorous stories, slang, and nonverbal expression to establish contact with them and win them to his client's cause. By the time he became junior partner to Logan, he was recognized as having, perhaps, the best "courtroom presence" in the Sangamon Bar.

During his years of partnership with Logan, Lincoln adopted many of the senior partner's good habits and became more methodical in preparation of his cases. The litigation Lincoln participated in was varied, but represented typical cases for lawyers of the Eighth Judicial Circuit. On the criminal side they varied from petty theft to murder, and they ran the entire gambit of civil cases. Lincoln frequently found himself in opposition to Stephen A. Douglas, who became state's attorney and an Illinois supreme court justice. In commenting on his courtroom battles with Lincoln, Douglas would later admit his tall opponent had "no equal before a jury."[20]

Lincoln, sometimes referred to as a "lawyer's lawyer," pleaded a number of cases before the Illinois Supreme Court in the 1840s. In *Bailey v. Cromwell* in 1841, Lincoln used the Northwest Ordinance of 1787 and the state constitution to successfully reverse a lower court decision and obtain freedom for a young Negro woman by the name of Nance. This case established the broad principle that "the presumption of the law in Illinois is that every person is free without regard to color" and "the sale of a free person is illegal."[21]

In December 1844, Lincoln and Logan terminated their partnership. Logan wanted to bring his son into the firm as junior partner, and Lincoln had gained sufficient reputation to start his own firm. Lincoln probably surprised everyone in the Sangamon Bar when he chose William Herndon as his partner. Herndon, who had been a clerk in the Logan and Lincoln office, was one of the less well known young men Lincoln could have chosen. He had only recently been accepted to the bar, and his personality left much to be desired. He was opinionated, self-centered, and undisciplined in both his drinking and professional habits. Herndon himself admitted he was surprised when Lincoln offered to make him a full partner.

Herndon's personal traits notwithstanding, he was a solid Whig in politics, and his age (he was nine years younger than Lincoln), helped the senior partner develop valuable relationships with the younger political activists of Springfield. Whatever Herndon's personal faults, he proved to be a loyal partner to Lincoln who did his best to promote the latter's professional and political advancement.

Robert Todd Lincoln,
age 17.

Library of Congress

Lincoln and Herndon developed a successful law practice, with the former generally handling the travelling duties on the Eighth Judicial Circuit and the latter staying in Springfield to run the office. They split the fees they received 50–50, which was quite generous to Herndon during the early years of their partnership and equally generous to Lincoln when he went away to Washington.

Lincoln and several other Whig politicians worked out an agreement in 1843 by which he and two others, John Hardin and Edward Baker, would take turns in running for the Seventh District's congressional seat. Hardin was first, and after successfully winning the election, served in Congress from

1843–1845. Baker was second, and served from 1845–1847. But when Lincoln's turn for the Whig nomination came, Hardin decided that he wanted to go back to Congress and attempted to maneuver him out of the Whig Party's nomination. Lincoln finally prevailed, and was selected to run against the Democratic nominee.

In March 1846, Mary gave birth to a second son, Edward Baker. Eddie, as he would be called, was named after Lincoln's friend and associate in the Sangamon Bar, Edward Baker.

Lincoln's Democratic opponent in the congressional race was Peter Cartwright, a well-known Methodist circuit rider and evangelist. As his campaign strategy, he took advantage of the fact that Lincoln was not a member of any Christian church to nurture the rumor that his opponent was an "infidel." Worried that Cartwright's efforts to discredit him might succeed, Lincoln published a handbill explaining his religious beliefs. There is a popular story of an interchange between the two candidates in church during the campaign. The evangelist, after failing to get a response from his opponent as to whether or not he wanted to go to heaven or hell, said, "May I inquire of you, Mr. Lincoln, where you are going?" "I am going to Congress," was Lincoln's reply.[22] He easily defeated Cartwright in the election and took his seat on December 6, 1847.

Mary, who accompanied Lincoln to Washington, found it difficult to adjust to life in the nation's capital. She believed people disliked her, and the winter weather kept her and the children indoors most of the time. Their accommodations at the Washington boardinghouse proved too small for the four of them, so in early March she took the boys and moved to Lexington, Kentucky to stay with her family.

Lincoln's two-year term in Congress was not very successful. The Mexican War was in progress, and soon after taking his seat, he attacked President James K. Polk in a series of arguments that became known as the "spot" resolutions. In these he tried to force the president to say whether American troops were on US soil when the first shots of the war were fired. Polk ignored the freshman congressman's questions, but Lincoln's constituents of the Seventh District in Illinois did not. The Springfield Democrats attempted to turn Lincoln's queries about the justification for the Mexican War into accusations that he was not supporting the troops. Although this was not true, Lincoln's reputation suffered back home.

Lincoln worked hard while in Congress. He faithfully accomplished party assignments, gave speeches, and performed countless favors for constituents. But with the exception of his 1849 bill to ban slavery in the District of Columbia, he did little that was historically noteworthy. This bill took the moderate approach of gradually abolishing slavery, but never became law. As a freshman Whig congressman, he was not able to assemble enough support to make formal submission of the bill worthwhile. Lincoln returned to Springfield at the end of his second session with no prospect of returning.

Having no desire to return to the state legislature, Lincoln rededicated himself to expanding his law practice. The Eighth Judicial Circuit, when Lincoln returned from Congress, included 14 counties and involved a four hundred-mile trek of 11 or 12 weeks. The spring term usually started in mid-March, and the fall term in early September. Most lawyers tried to minimize the time away from their families by either heading home Saturday to spend Sunday with them, or dividing circuit duty with their partners. But Lincoln usually found an excuse to stay away from home on the weekends and did not split circuit work with Herndon. According to Eighth Circuit Judge David Davis, the unspoken understanding among the lawyers was that Lincoln's home life with Mary was not pleasant.

The circuit courts drew large crowds. In some county seats, such as Logan County's tiny Mt. Pulaski, there was little in the way of established entertainment for the local people other than the bi-annual drama of the circuit court. People seemed to enjoy the courtroom antics, even if it amounted to little more than a bunch of shrewd out-of-town lawyers arguing over the ownership of a litter of pigs.

Circuit life was physically grueling. The circuit riders would travel for hours at a time in their buggies or on horseback on terrible roads, through all kinds of weather. Judge Davis usually led the caravan of the state's attorney and 25 or 30 lawyers into town on Sunday or Monday. They had a day or two to communicate with clients and their local counsel, prepare pleadings, and get ready for the opening of court mid-week. Court week might last only a few days, or as much as two weeks. When the docket was cleared everyone headed out for the next county seat, which was usually at least a day's ride away.

Lincoln spent four or five months a year in this regime, eating mediocre food, living in hotels, and sharing a bedroom with three or four other lawyers. Although it was very tiresome, Lincoln never complained and only missed two rotations of the circuit in nearly 11 years. Evening entertainment usually consisted of meeting in the hotel parlor, telling jokes and swapping stories. This was something at which Lincoln excelled, and Judge Davis became a close friend of Lincoln during these years.

The Lincoln's son Eddie died in February 1850, and, seeking solace, Mary joined the First Presbyterian Church of Springfield. Although Lincoln did not formally join the church himself, he attended regularly with Mary and rented a family pew. During this time of his life, Lincoln became a serious student of the Gospel, developing an even stronger belief in predestination. It became increasingly his philosophy that man should strive to know the will of God, so that he could pray and act in accordance with that will. This desire to comply with God's plans, as opposed to petitioning

William Wallace (Willie) Lincoln, whose tragic death in the White House was a significant shock to his parents.

Courtesy of the Illinois State Historical Library

Thomas (Tadd) Lincoln, in a soldier's uniform made for him while in the White House.

National Archives

God to comply with man's, became one of Lincoln's strongest beliefs. He would later say, "Whatever shall appear to be God's will, I will do."[23]

Mary, who had gone through a serious bout of depression when Eddie died, was cheered by the birth of their third son, William Wallace, in December 1850. Later known as Willie, he would become the most amicable and cheerful of the Lincoln boys. Willie was followed by the Lincoln's fourth son, Thomas, born in 1853. Thomas would become known as "Tad," and his slight speech impediment would cause the two boys to grow very close over the next few years. Willie took it as his personal responsibility to help his younger brother communicate with others.

From 1849 to 1854 Lincoln put most of his time into his law practice, but he always kept apprised of what was going on in the field of his first love, politics. He maintained correspondence with various political contacts, continued to make speeches, and, even though he did not run for any office, he tried to keep a prominent role in the Illinois political scene. He might have continued in this vein and remained nothing more than a successful prairie lawyer for the rest of his life if it weren't for an event that took place in Washington, D.C. This event would be the passage of Stephen A. Douglas' Kansas-Nebraska Act in 1854.

Spokesman

Abraham Lincoln rose from his chair on the speaker's stand very slowly. He pulled himself up to his full height, nearly six feet four inches, and nodded politely to the cheering crowd. With the shouts of the boisterous audience ringing in his ears, a wistful smile came to his lips. The melancholy look in his eyes quickly vanished, and he was transformed from a man whose mind seemed a thousand miles away to one that was conscious he had the most important of tasks before him. He turned, walked quickly to the speaker's podium, and faced the audience. The occasion was Lincoln's reply to Stephen A. Douglas' opening speech during the last of the Lincoln-Douglas debates in Alton, Illinois, on October 15, 1858.

Lincoln raised his hands to quiet the audience. With a twinkle in his eye, he began the way the crowd loved most—by poking fun at the somber Douglas. He said that he had been "complimented" by his adversary, and was glad to see that Judge Douglas was making progress in his political fight against President Buchanan. He was referring to Douglas' split with the leader of the Democratic Party, President James Buchanan, over the issue of allowing Kansas to be admitted as a slave state. Buchanan insisted on admitting Kansas as a slave state under the Lecompton State Constitution—one that had been fraudulently approved by a pro-slavery minority. Douglas believed this was not in accordance with the spirit of Popular Sovereignty, and insisted on ratification of a new state constitution.

Lincoln said that the feud between Douglas and Buchanan reminded him of the old woman who, in watching her husband fight a bear, decided she had better not take sides because of the uncertainty of who would win. So, in watching the two democrats fight over Lecompton, Lincoln felt like shouting what the old woman said: "Go it, husband! Go it, bear!"

This had the desired effect of bringing uproarious laughter from the crowd and a scowl from the judge, who had to once again watch the advantages he'd gained from a well-researched argument crumble before the homely antics of his shrewd opponent.

Having gained the audience's rapt attention, Lincoln quickly changed from comic to skilled debater. He reviewed previous statements of Judge Douglas, and high-lighted both differences and similarities in their respective positions on slavery. He said "the real issue in this controversy . . . [is] the sentiment on the part of one class that looks upon slavery as a wrong, and the other class that does not look upon it as a wrong." People nodded in agreement. Lincoln was well known for his ability to present complicated arguments in a simple way that could be understood by everyone.

The history of slavery legislation in America was familiar to most people in the 1850s. The most important legislation had been the Missouri Compromise of 1820. It had limited slavery's expansion into the new territories by precluding admission of new slave states, with the exception of Missouri, above the latitude of 36 degrees 30 minutes. This constraint caused people to believe that fewer slave states would be admitted from the territories, the pro-slavery bloc would lose power in the Senate, and slavery would eventually die.

Next came the Compromise of 1850, which successfully diffused the crisis over territory acquired during the War with Mexico. However, it was the Kansas-Nebraska Act of 1854 that changed everything. This act repealed the Missouri Compromise and declared that the residents of any territory, regardless of whether or not they were north of latitude 36 degrees, 30 minutes, had a right to decide for themselves if their state would enter the Union as free or slave. This concept, called "Popular Sovereignty" by its democratic sponsor, Stephen A. Douglas, was supported by many of the Southern slave holders.

Douglas, who introduced Popular Sovereignty in order to gain political favor with the South, did not reckon on the furor his Kansas-Nebraska Act caused. It propelled slavery from a background issue—of interest to only the Northern abolitionists and the Southern fire-eaters—to one that virtually everyone, including the politically dormant Abraham Lincoln, became interested in.

Although Lincoln hated slavery, he recognized the magnitude of the slave states' political power and realized there would be no peaceful means of quickly eliminating the institution. Consequently, he supported the Missouri Compromise's limitations to the spread of slavery, and believed it the best way of both eliminating slavery and averting war. He was afraid the Kansas-Nebraska Act would have the effect of expanding, rather than gradually strangling, slavery in the territories.

He developed a theory that there was a secret conspiracy by the Democratic Party to propagate, rather than limit, slavery. He joined the new Republican Party, which was antislavery, and in 1856 made a number of political speeches throughout the Midwest, arguing against the Kansas-Nebraska Act.

In addition to the Kansas-Nebraska Act, another major setback for antislavery forces was the Supreme Court's 1857 Dred Scott Decision. Dred Scott, a slave, had sued for his freedom based on his temporary residence in a free state. The Supreme Court declared that as a black man, Scott had no rights—and could not bring suit for his freedom in a court of law. This decision was supported by the Democratic Party, and Stephen A. Douglas proclaimed it to be the final answer to the question on the legality of slavery in the territories. He encouraged everyone to accept it as the ultimate decision of the "highest tribunal of the land."

Lincoln refused to support the Supreme Court's decision in this action. The Dred Scott decision strengthened his conviction that major powers in the government, specifically President Buchanan, Supreme Court Chief Justice Roger Taney, and Democratic Party congressional leadership, including Stephen A. Douglas, were conspiring to propagate slavery into both the new territories and existing free states.

In 1858, Stephen A. Douglas' term in the Senate was up, and Lincoln received the Illinois Republican Party's nomination to run against him in the fall election. Having argued bills with Lincoln in the state legislature and law with him in various courtrooms, Douglas was well acquainted with the tall Republican. When Douglas was asked if Lincoln would be an easy opponent to defeat, he replied in the negative. "I shall have my hands full," Douglas warned. "He is the strong man of his party—full of wit, facts, dates—and the best stump speaker, with his droll ways and dry jokes, in the West."[24]

Lincoln and Douglas met in seven different locations during the debates. Sometimes referred to as the Great Debates, these were in the Illinois towns of Freeport, Ottawa, Quincy, Galesburg, Jonesboro, Charleston, and Alton. Douglas used every tactic he could to fight the "Black Republican," which was a derogatory term for members of the new antislavery party. One of his favorite methods of attack was to declare that when freedom was granted to African Americans, they would attain equal social status with white people and begin intermarrying with them. The concept of equal social status with black people was offensive to white audiences in the 1850s, and Lincoln was careful to avoid any appearance of supporting this.

Citing the fact that slaves were present at the time of the Revolutionary War, Douglas stated the black man was not considered by the authors of the Declaration of Independence. He believed the statement "all men are created equal" did not include African Americans.

Lincoln, on the other hand, believed the authors of the Declaration included African Americans in the statement "all men are created equal," but that they did not think them equal in all respects to white people. He believed that they thought slavery was a moral wrong , but wanted to allow it to continue until an unspecified future date when the slaves would be granted freedom.

Lincoln stated that the primary issue of the day was whether or not slavery was a moral wrong. He argued that if the black man was a human being, and the Declaration of Independence was right, then slavery was wrong and should be abolished. He condemned Stephen A. Douglas' lack of concern about the morality of slavery, and believed that if the people ignored this moral issue they would one day pay a terrible price.

Lincoln lost the senate election to Douglas. This was because in the 1850s, senators were chosen by the state legislatures rather than direct vote of the people. Although more pro-Lincoln legislators won office in this election, the Democrats had a hold-over majority in the General Assembly.

In April of 1859, Lincoln started to consider running for president of the United States. Like many other successful candidates, he began by publicly denying his worthiness for the office. He wrote "I do not think myself fit for the Presidency" to more than one correspondent in the spring of 1859.[25]

By the time of the Republican National Convention in May 1860, Lincoln was actively seeking his party's nomination. Although William H. Seward, former governor of New York, had been expected to become the Republican Party's nominee, during his tenure as the Republican frontrunner he acquired more enemies than friends. Thanks to this fact, plus some skillful caucusing of delegates by floor manager Judge David Davis, Lincoln defeated Seward at the Republican Convention on May 18, 1860, and became his party's candidate for president.

Although few people knew much about Lincoln, most realized the Republican nominee had an excellent chance of becoming the next president. The Democratic Party had split over the slavery issue, with Southern Democrats insisting on assurance that slavery would always be protected in the new territories and Northern Democrats refusing to go along with this. The Southern Democrats nominated John Breckinridge of Kentucky and the Northern Democrats chose Stephen A. Douglas.

In addition to the two democrats, Lincoln's opposition was further diluted by a fourth candidate, John Bell of Tennessee, who as a Constitutional Unionist was supported by die-hard Whigs and former Know-Nothings. As a result of this division, Lincoln won the election on a platform that pledged to keep slavery out of the new territories, but not to affect it where it currently existed.

Refusing to accept a president that might eventually threaten slavery, Southern leaders and proslavery advocates called for state conventions in South Carolina, Mississippi, Florida, Alabama, Georgia, Louisiana, and

Texas. These conventions passed ordinances of secession and sent representatives to Montgomery, Alabama to draw up a constitution for a new
government they called the Confederate States of America. They elected
Jefferson Davis of Mississippi president on February 18, 1861.

Lincoln went to the Springfield train depot on February 11, 1861, to
board the special train that was waiting to take him to Washington. He
ascended the rear platform, turned to face the audience, and took off his
hat. He stood for several minutes, silently facing the quiet crowd, and men
in the audience took off their hats also, in spite of a steady rain. Finally,
with a voice choked by emotion, he reminisced about his life in Springfield
and thanked his friends for all they had done for him. He wondered aloud
whether or not he would ever return. In closing he asked them to pray for
him, because he believed he was about to undertake a task that was even
greater than the one that had fallen upon President Washington.

The train took 12 days to complete the trip to Washington. The reason
the trip was long was so Lincoln could stop at various towns and cities
along the way and give the people an opportunity to see him. He made
many brief speeches, most of which demonstrated his trust in God and
confidence in the people's ability to resolve the crisis. When he reached
Philadelphia he learned there was a plot to assassinate him in Baltimore.
Consequently he and a few trusted men made an overnight trip through
Maryland in order to avoid trouble. He arrived in Washington on February 23 and began his final preparations for the inauguration.

The Leader

*President-elect Abraham Lincoln and President James Buchanan emerged from
the swearing-in ceremony of Vice President Hannibal Hamlin and walked out
onto the platform erected at the Capitol's east portico. The audience offered polite
applause, and Lincoln was introduced by his old friend, Senator Edward Baker.
Rising to give his inaugural address, Lincoln paused awkwardly and looked around
for a place to put his hat. As the crowd of 25,000 waited, Lincoln's old rival Stephen
A. Douglas stepped forward and offered to hold the hat for him. Lincoln put on his
reading glasses, unfolded the paper, and looked out upon the audience. He could
see at the edge of the crowd the soldiers and cannon General Winfield Scott had put
in place to enforce the old soldiers' pledge to "manure the hills of Arlington" with
the fragments of any person trying to interrupt the inauguration.*

*Lincoln spoke for half an hour, delivering one of the most memorable inaugural
addresses in the history of the Republic. In it he attempted to do the impossible and
convince the Southern people that they had neither cause nor right to secede from
the Union. He appealed to their reason, their patriotism, and finally to their abhor-
rence of war. He told them that the issue of Civil War was in their hands, not his.
He made a final appeal to "the better angels of our nature," and stopped. Chief
Justice Roger Taney, who presided over the Supreme Court that handed down the*

Dred Scott Decision, shuffled forward and administered the oath of office. Abraham Lincoln, 16th President of the United States, bowed his head and kissed the Bible.

Fort Sumter was Lincoln's first major crisis after becoming president. The fort, on an island in the middle of South Carolina's Charleston harbor, was garrisoned by less than one hundred Federal soldiers. Thousands of Confederate troops surrounded the fort with cannon and demanded its surrender.

Lincoln, in a manner that would later be considered uncharacteristic, was indecisive. He repeatedly solicited the advice of his cabinet regarding Fort Sumter. Most of them, plus the chief of the army, Winfield Scott, advised him to surrender it. But Lincoln, who had sworn in his inaugural address to defend government property, was reluctant to give it up.

Ignoring the majority of his advisors, Lincoln decided against abandonment of Fort Sumter, and advised Confederate President Jefferson Davis that he would send ships to provide the garrison with food and water. Davis elected to attack rather than allow the post to be resupplied, and consequently the Confederacy fired the first shots of the war on April 12, 1861. Fort Sumter soon surrendered and its soldiers were sent home.

The firing on Fort Sumter enraged the people of the North and united them in support of the Union. On April 15 Lincoln called for 75,000 volunteers to join the army and suppress the rebellion. The Northern authorities had to turn away thousands in excess of that number, and troops were soon encamped around Washington, preparing for war.

Subsequent to Lincoln's call for volunteers, the states of Virginia, Arkansas, North Carolina, and Tennessee seceded and joined the Confederate States. The Southern capital was moved from Montgomery, Alabama to Richmond, Virginia—merely one hundred miles from Washington, D.C.

On July 4, Lincoln called a special session of Congress to ask for approval of several emergency war measures he had already put in place. Congress eventually approved Lincoln's emergency measures, which included a temporary suspension of habeas corpus in several regions of Maryland. It also allowed expansion of the armed forces and provided funds for the prosecution of the war.[26]

As commander in chief, one of Lincoln's most important tasks was leading the war effort. When he took office, he inherited a peacetime army of about 16,000 men that was led by the aged Winfield Scott—hero of the War of 1812 and the Mexican War. Scott was too old and overweight to ride a horse, so Brigadier General Irvin McDowell took field command of the volunteers. Many of the troops had enlisted for only 90 days, so Lincoln was forced to use them by the middle of the summer before their enlistments were up.

Consequently, the unfortunate McDowell had to lead the unprepared army southward towards the enemy. They departed on July 16, approximately 35,000 strong, and were followed by dozens of civilians that planned to picnic and watch the expected battle. At Manassas, Virginia they fought 32,000 Confederate troops commanded by generals Pierre G. T. Beauregard and Joseph E. Johnston . After a hard fight, the Northern army was routed and retreated all the way to Washington.

Within a few days, Lincoln replaced McDowell with Major General George B. McClellan. McClellan had led a successful military campaign in the mountains of western Virginia, and soon arrived in Washington, exuding confidence and success. A superb organizer, over the next several months he transformed the demoralized mob of soldiers into a confident, proud force of men that became known as "The Army of the Potomac."

After the shock of the defeat at Manassas, Lincoln recognized the country's need for prayer and encouragement, and made his first Proclamation of a National Fast Day on August 12, 1861. In it he said, "it is peculiarly fit for us to recognize the hand of God in this terrible visitation . . . and to pray for His mercy."[27]

Realizing he was ignorant of military strategy, Lincoln took the extraordinary step of checking out books from the Library of Congress and attempted to educate himself on the topic, much as he had done with various other subjects. In addition to this, he developed a close relationship with the soldiers, and was sometimes seen mingling with troops encamped on the White House grounds, swapping stories and passing out drinks of water. Trusting in his common sense and own judge of character, Lincoln began to hire and fire his commanding generals with little or no counsel from anyone, including the secretary of war.

In February of 1862, tragedy struck the Lincoln family. Their 11-year-old son, Willie, fell ill with fever and died. Both Lincoln and Mary were terribly overcome with grief. After Willie's death, Lincoln developed a closer relationship with Reverend Phineas D. Gurley of the New York Avenue Presbyterian Church, and began to attend church more frequently. During Wednesday evening prayer services he usually sat in a room adjacent to the sanctuary, where he could listen to the sermon without being seen by the congregation.

Unfortunately for the North's war effort, General McClellan proved a master at delaying battle. He refused to attack the Confederates until confident his army was completely prepared, and from the summer of 1861 until the spring of 1862, newspapers and magazines continuously proclaimed "all quiet on the Potomac." McClellan, who was excessively cautious by nature, always believed he was grossly outnumbered by the enemy. No matter how many troops or supplies Lincoln provided him, McClellan wanted more. Lincoln once said that sending troops to

McClellan was like "shoveling fleas across the barnyard—half of them never get there."[28]

While McClellan delayed in the East, a little-known brigadier general by the name of Ulysses S. Grant took a force of gunboats and troops up the Tennessee and Cumberland Rivers in Kentucky and captured two Confederate forts. At one of them, Fort Donelson, he captured 13,000 Confederate soldiers and caused a collapse of the Confederate defenses in middle Kentucky and Tennessee.

These successes in February and March of 1862 were followed by a near disaster in April. Grant's army was surprised at Pittsburg Landing, Tennessee, by a Confederate army under General Albert Sidney Johnston. In what would eventually become known as the Battle of Shiloh, Grant narrowly defeated the Confederates in what was up to then the bloodiest battle on the American continent. When powerful political leaders demanded Grant's resignation, Lincoln refused. "I can't spare this man; he fights," he said.[29]

In March 1862, McClellan finally began a powerful offensive against the Southern army. Using an armada of ships, he moved his army down Chesapeake Bay and landed it on the Virginia peninsula between the York and James Rivers, east of Richmond. Hauling up massive siege guns and moving cautiously, McClellan slowly advanced to within a few miles of the Southern capital. His opponents, Confederate generals Joseph E. Johnston and Robert E. Lee, took advantage of McClellan's overcautiousness. In a series of daring attacks, known today as the Seven Days battles, Lee soon forced the Northern army to retreat from the gates of Richmond and take refuge along the James River shoreline.

The spring and summer of 1862 were difficult days for the Lincoln administration. In April, hope had been high that McClellan would capture Richmond and end the war. But by late summer, Lee had defeated McClellan. As a result of the military reverse, Lincoln was denounced by both political parties, but maintained his resolve to save the Union.

While McClellan was clinging to the banks of the James River, with a superior army and powerful Union gunboats at his disposal, Lee seized the initiative and marched north. Lincoln had assembled a second army in northern Virginia, put it under the command of Major General John Pope, and brought one of his generals from the Western Theatre, Major General Henry Halleck, east to become the North's general in chief. But Lee defeated Pope on the old Manassas battlefield in late August, before McClellan and most of the Army of the Potomac could be brought back to reinforce him. Lee prepared to invade Maryland.

Lee's invasion was a tremendous crisis for the Union, and there is evidence that it caused Lincoln to contemplate God's purposes for the war and what his own actions should be. He believed that God was allowing the war to go on for some mysterious purpose known only to Himself, and concluded he should pray to find the course that would comply with God's will.

Lincoln ordered McClellan's troops back to the Washington area and put McClellan in command of the combined forces of his and Pope's armies. Many political leaders objected to Lincoln's re-instatement of McClellan to command of the forces around Washington. But Lincoln recognized the demoralization of the soldiers, and knew the general's presence would be a great boost to morale. When Senator Ben Wade of Ohio said that he would put "anybody" in command except McClellan, Lincoln replied, "Wade, *any*body will do for you, but not for me. I must have *some*body." [30] Lincoln's judgment proved correct, and the troops were ecstatic when they found out that McClellan, not Pope, commanded them. The Army of the Potomac marched northward, staying between Lee and Washington.

By the summer of 1862, Lincoln had developed a close relationship with the famous black abolitionist, Frederick Douglass. Douglass was an outspoken advocate of not only freeing the slaves, but also allowing black men to join the army in order to fight for the Union. Although Douglass wanted Lincoln to act more quickly in freeing the slaves than he did, he nevertheless developed a great respect for the president. Douglass said:

"I was impressed by his [Lincoln's] entire freedom from popular prejudice against the colored race." He was the first "great" man Douglass had ever met "who in no single instance reminded me of the difference between himself and myself, of the difference of color." [31]

Up to this time, Lincoln held the position that the war was strictly for the purpose of maintaining the Union, and not to free the slaves. Although he hated slavery "as much as any abolitionist," [32] he believed that his primary duty as president was to preserve the government of the United States, and feared that any premature effort to free the slaves would cause the states of Kentucky, Missouri, and Maryland to join the Confederacy. He also feared, early in the war, that many Union soldiers would refuse to fight if the purpose of the war was to end slavery.

In the summer of 1862, Lincoln decided the majority of the people would probably support him if he added freedom for the slaves to the war's objectives. Although adding abolition of slavery was somewhat of a gamble, he believed that it would provide both immediate and long term benefits. An immediate benefit would be the elimination of the threat that Britain may enter the war on the side of the Confederacy—which was something she was increasingly tempted to do. Britain was interested in a Confederate victory, and as long as abrogation of slavery was not a war aim of the North, the British government could not be accused of any lack of morality if it intervened on behalf of the South. But if Lincoln added emancipation to his war objectives, Britain could no longer morally justify support to the South.

Another immediate benefit of ending slavery was a rekindling of purpose for the Northern people. Slavery had always been something that most Northerners were uncomfortable with, but the majority had ignored it because they knew that in order to maintain harmony with the South, they had to let it continue. But the South was now the enemy, and attacking slavery would not only have the short term benefit of weakening the Southern states, but also the long term benefit of destroying an institution that was considered a moral evil.

Lincoln still had legitimate concern that many Northern people would not support the destruction of slavery as a war purpose. He knew that abolitionists would be ecstatic about the change, but they were the minority, and he sought an opportunity to show the majority a practical reason for freeing the slaves. Horace Greeley, editor of the New York *Tribune*, presented him this opportunity when he challenged the president to respond to an editorial entitled "The Prayer of Twenty Millions." In his response, published in the *Tribune*, Lincoln declared his primary purpose in the war was to save the Union, and pointed out that freeing the slaves might be helpful in doing this.

In the summer of 1862, Lincoln first proposed the idea of freeing the slaves to his cabinet. They were surprised by this, and during the ensuing discussion convinced him that it would be best to postpone this action. Seward suggested that they should announce emancipation after a military victory, because to announce it while the Northern armies were on retreat would sound like an act of desperation.

When Lee invaded the North, McClellan sought to protect the capital by keeping the Army of the Potomac between the Confederate army and Washington. The Northern commander moved cautiously, not certain as to whether Lee was going to attack Baltimore or Washington. Lincoln feared that McClellan would again prove no match for Lee, and it seemed a gift from God when Northern soldiers found a copy of Lee's invasion plans lying in a field. McClellan, who was suddenly emboldened, decided to attack Lee while the Southern army was geographically dispersed.

Even though he knew Lee's plans, McClellan still moved so slowly that Lee was able to concentrate his forces before being attacked. On September 17, 1862, the two armies fought the most costly one-day battle in American history along Antietam Creek near Sharpsburg, Maryland. More than 23,000 men were killed, wounded, or captured in a fight that would be known as the Battle of Antietam. Lee was forced to return to Virginia, and Lincoln had the victory he was waiting for. Five days after the battle Lincoln issued the preliminary Emancipation Proclamation, announcing it would take effect in those states remaining in rebellion at the beginning of the new year.

Although many people in the North rejected the idea of freeing the slaves, the soldiers kept fighting. Most of the men were growing tired of the war and welcomed the idea of black soldiers coming to help. Consequently, in getting past the nation's previous resistance on the emancipation issue, Lincoln successfully transformed the war's purpose from one with the single purpose of maintaining the Union to one that was also to free the slaves.[33]

Lincoln believed that as commander in chief he possessed the authority to use whatever means was necessary to destroy the enemies of the United States. Consequently he issued the Emancipation Proclamation as a war measure—freeing slaves of the regions in rebellion. Although the immediate term impact on slavery was limited, it had significant long term impact. Once the Union armies started marching through the deep South, the institution of slavery was doomed. Thousands of slaves would leave their masters and follow the Yankee soldiers.

On October 19, Lincoln appointed his old friend from the Illinois Eighth Judicial Circuit, Judge David Davis, to a vacancy on the Supreme Court. Lincoln was pleased to do a favor for the man that had probably done more than anyone else to win Lincoln the Republican Party's nomination for the presidency in 1860.

Lincoln recognized after the Battle of Antietam that simply driving the Southern army from Maryland was not enough. He insisted that McClellan move south and attack Lee, but the general was up to his old habit of delay. An obviously frustrated Lincoln telegraphed: "Major-General McClellan: I have just read your dispatch about sore-tongued and fatigued horses. Will you pardon me for asking what the horses of your army have done since the battle of Antietam that fatigue anything?"[34]

Lincoln decided that if McClellan let Lee reach central Virginia without attacking him, he would remove him from command of the army. McClellan allowed Lee to escape and on November 5, 1862, Lincoln dismissed McClellan and replaced him with Major General Ambrose Burnside.

In December 1862 the Army of the Potomac was badly mauled when General Burnside attacked Lee in a strongly fortified position in Fredericksburg, Virginia. Recognizing the damage Burnside had done to the morale of the army, Lincoln replaced him with another officer from the Army of the Potomac, Major General Joseph Hooker. Lincoln sent the new commander a letter, advising him of the reasons he had been placed in command. In this letter, Lincoln frankly told Hooker what he did and did not like about him. He also provided some sound advice on how to prosecute the war. Hooker, rather than being insulted by this letter, was deeply touched. He stated that it was the sort of letter "a father might write to his son" and treasured it.[35] Like most men of the Union armies, he had developed respect and affection for Lincoln.

The Statesman

President Lincoln sat on the speaker's platform, surrounded by the dignitaries that were in charge of the dedication ceremony. He listened patiently to the closing statements of the famous orator Edward Everett, who had delivered a two-hour-long speech for the occasion—the dedication of the Soldiers National Cemetery in Gettysburg, Pennsylvania. When Mr. Everett finished, the president joined the audience in polite applause, and then grasped the hand of the famous orator and personally thanked him. After everyone sang a short hymn, Mr. Lincoln was introduced to the audience by his friend Ward Lamon, grand marshal of the ceremonies.

Standing in the center of the platform, and unfolding the pieces of paper on which he had written what he called a "few appropriate remarks," Lincoln waited patiently for the applause to subside. People were not certain of what to expect. Everett, the keynote speaker, had provided them with an emotional, picturesque account of the battle and events that had taken place on that field four months ago. As was customary for celebrated speakers of that day, he delivered a long, memorized speech, and the people stood quietly and listened patiently to every word.

Lincoln's message was short and simple. He began by reminding his audience of what the nation's founders had accomplished nearly a century before. He said they had established a nation that was dedicated to a proposed idea, not yet a proven fact, that all men are created equal. He stated they were gathered in Gettysburg to honor the lives of men that had died so that the nation would live. He closed by encouraging them to devote themselves to the same cause for which the men had died—that the nation would have a "new birth of freedom" and that government of the people would survive.

With this short speech, Lincoln linked the soldiers' sacrifice with the Declaration of Independence's statement about equality, in addition to the Constitution. Lincoln subtly revealed, in about 270 words, what he would accomplish as president— the transformation of the war's purpose. The war that had begun with the single goal to maintain the Union would end with a second goal added—the elimination of slavery.[36]

General Joseph Hooker proved to be an excellent organizer of men, and soon had the Army of the Potomac ready for battle. He conceived an excellent plan to defeat Lee, and if he had carried it through to completion, may very well have succeeded. But Lee proved the bolder general, and Hooker was defeated at the battle of Chancellorsville in late spring of 1863. Lee's victory was paid for at a terrible price when his most dynamic military commander, Lieutenant General T. J. "Stonewall" Jackson, died.

Although Hooker was defeated, the Army of the Potomac was not. Many of the troops under his command were never put into battle at all.

With Hooker's defeat, there was again a short reprieve in the fighting, while each commander considered his next move.

In addition to the military maneuvers, one of Lincoln's greatest concerns as commander in chief had to do with soldiers sentenced to be shot for desertion. Lincoln, who could easily have ignored these sentences, was not the type of leader to do so. He had compassion for these men, and claimed that he did not know for certain he might not run away too, if put in similar circumstances. Consequently, he required all capital cases to be sent to him for review before sentences could be carried out. He stayed up late at night and went through these cases, searching each for an excuse to pardon the condemned. Lincoln understood his generals when they complained his pardons undermined military discipline, but in situations like this his heart ruled his mind.[37]

While the eastern army commanders were fumbling against Lee, Ulysses S. Grant continued to win victories in the West. Grant, assisted by navy gunboats, had opened up the Mississippi River all the way to Vicksburg by the spring of 1863. Although Grant's army was delayed by Confederate cannon on the bluffs of Vicksburg for many months, he finally forced his way past the guns and landed his troops below the city. Vicksburg fell to Grant on July 4, 1863.

Lee took advantage of Hooker's inaction after Chancellorsville and invaded the North a second time. Recognizing that his army commander was a defeated man, Lincoln took the bold step of replacing him with a new commander, Major General George G. Meade, only a few days before the Battle of Gettysburg.

Maintaining the defensive, Meade and the Army of the Potomac defeated Lee at the Battle of Gettysburg, Pennsylvania on July 3, 1863. Over 50,000 Americans were killed, wounded, or captured in this three-day fight. Lee's losses, more than half of this total, were severe enough that he and the Army of Northern Virginia were never again able to mount a major offensive operation.

In addition to his problems with generals, Lincoln's leadership skills were frequently tested when dealing with his presidential cabinet. Several of the cabinet members, especially Secretary of State William H. Seward and Secretary of the Treasury Salmon P. Chase, had been strong political rivals of Lincoln before the war. Seward considered himself a better leader, and tried to dominate the president in the early months of the war. Lincoln proved to be the more capable, however, and Seward soon admitted that "the president is the best of us."[38] He and Lincoln became close friends.

But Salmon P. Chase was a constant annoyance to Lincoln. He attempted to enlist the aid of several powerful members of the Senate against his chief, complaining that Lincoln rarely consulted his cabinet. Chase also stirred up a movement to have Seward removed from his position as secretary of state. Lincoln outmaneuvered his subordinate, however, and kept both of the secretaries in their cabinet positions. It wasn't until late in the war, when Chase failed in his effort to supersede Lincoln as the Republican nominee for the presidency, that he finally decided to accept the secretary of the treasury's resignation. Never one to hold a grudge, he later appointed Chase to the United States Supreme Court.

Another headstrong cabinet member was the secretary of war, Edwin Stanton. Stanton, who was also a lawyer, had been co-counsel with Lincoln in an important lawsuit before the war. Stanton refused to cooperate with Lincoln on the case, and even called him an insulting name. But this did not keep Lincoln from selecting Stanton for his cabinet when he decided to replace the original secretary of war, Simon Cameron. Lincoln knew Stanton would be an able administrator, and in him soon developed a loyal subordinate.

In October 1863, Lincoln placed Grant in overall command in the Western Theatre and sent him to take charge of the Union army that was under siege in Chattanooga, Tennessee. Grant defeated the Confederates at Chattanooga on November 25, 1863, and Lincoln brought him east to take command of all Union armies.

With Grant, Lincoln finally had a commanding general that believed in prosecuting the war as aggressively as he did. Like Lincoln, Grant believed in simultaneous attacks by all armies on all fronts. With Grant in the East, and the aggressive William Tecumseh Sherman commanding in Georgia, Lincoln had commanders that understood victory would be simply a matter of continuous application of overwhelming military force.

Grant attacked Lee on May 5, 1864, on virtually the same ground that Hooker had a year earlier. When halted by Lee in the Battle of the Wilderness, Grant simply went around Lee's flank and continued to press southward. Sherman, meanwhile, advanced towards Atlanta, using flanking maneuvers to put his foe, General Joseph E. Johnston, in retreat. But the advance south for Grant and Sherman was slow, costly work.

One of Lincoln's Springfield friends, Joshua Speed, visited Lincoln in the summer of 1864. When Speed walked into the room, and saw Lincoln reading the Bible, he purportedly said to him, "I am glad to see you profitably engaged." Lincoln replied, "Yes, I *am* profitably engaged." "Well," Speed said, "if you have recovered from your skepticism, I am sorry to say that I have not." Lincoln looked Speed earnestly in the face, and placed his hand on his shoulder. He then said, "You are wrong, Speed. Take all of this Book upon reason that you can and the balance on faith, and you will live and die a happier and better man."[39]

The battle casualties continued to rise, especially in the East, and by the end of the summer many Northern people were demanding an end to war. By late August, neither Richmond nor Atlanta had fallen, and Lincoln became concerned he would be defeated in the fall presidential election. George B. McClellan had been nominated as the Democratic Party's candidate and was beginning to appeal to war-weary citizens. The Democrats were hinting they would be willing to negotiate peace and let the South form a separate nation. Lincoln desperately needed a military victory to prevent this from happening.

Lincoln proclaimed two days of National Thanksgiving and Prayer, first on September 3, 1864, and then on October 20. About this time he wrote to a Quaker friend, expressing both his belief that "the purposes of the Almighty are perfect," and his gratefulness for the people's prayers.[40]

William T. Sherman provided the North with a crucial victory when he captured Atlanta on September 2, 1864. Thanks to this victory, plus a significant victory by Philip H. Sheridan at Winchester, Virginia, the threat to Lincoln's re-election evaporated almost overnight. He easily defeated McClellan in the November elections.

In spite of the fact that the Army of the Potomac's former commander had been Lincoln's democratic opponent, the soldier vote went solidly for Lincoln. Most of them voted for Lincoln not only because the president was popular, but also they could not stand the thought of allowing the South to secede after the sacrifice of so many comrades' lives. Everyone recognized that Lincoln was a leader that was committed to winning the war.

Grant had continuously forced Lee's army to retreat until mid-summer of 1864, when he at last had established a siegelike position on the outskirts of Richmond. The two armies entrenched near the city of Petersburg, Virginia and began the slow process of trench warfare. Grant continued to extend his lines west and southward, trying to outflank Lee, and the latter continuously extended his lines to meet each new threat. This process continued from the summer into the winter months, with the Confederate army growing continuously weaker and the Union army stronger.

After taking Atlanta in early September, Sherman evacuated civilians from the city and burned all military stores and facilities that would be useful to the Confederacy. He then sent part of his army back to Nashville, Tennessee to guard against an invasion of the North. He took the remainder of his army, about 60,000 troops, and marched from Atlanta to Savannah, cutting a 60-mile-wide swath of destruction across the state of Georgia.

Sherman arrived at Savannah shortly before Christmas, and after re-equipping his troops and taking a short rest, started marching northward through the Carolinas. The Confederate army that opposed him was a motley collection of less than 30,000 soldiers, many of whom were old men and young boys. Even though they were commanded by the capable Joseph E. Johnston, they were unable to present any serious opposition to Sherman's battle-hardened troops, and he continued to press towards Virginia.

Meanwhile General John Bell Hood, now in command of the army of 39,000 that had evacuated Atlanta, marched northward. After a costly battle at Franklin, Tennessee on November 30, they arrived on the outskirts of Nashville. Facing Hood was the capable Union General George H. Thomas and an army of nearly 70,000 Federal troops. Thomas attacked Hood on December 15 and 16 and almost totally annihilated the Confederate army. By January 1, 1865, virtually every Confederate force, with the exception of Lee's in Virginia and E. Kirby Smith's west of the Mississippi, had ceased to be a viable threat to the Union forces that faced them.

Lincoln began his second term of office on March 4, 1865. With his second inaugural address, he presented an extremely well-thought-out document that explained his beliefs in the reason for the war, God's purposes for the same, and what the country must do to compensate for its failures. Described as "a sacred effort" by the abolitionist Frederick Douglass, it exhibited the mind of a leader that had deeply contemplated the Bible, Divine will, and man's responsibility to God.

After Lincoln's second inaugural, it was obvious to everyone that victory for the North was simply a matter of time. Lincoln was confident that the Union would survive and the Confederate States would be forced to both return to the Union and emancipate the slaves. Lee's army continued to grow weaker because of a worsening supply situation and increasing troop desertions. Lee finally decided to make one last strike at a strong point in Grant's lines known as Fort Stedman and retreat towards North Carolina. His hope was that he could get to the mountains, unite with Joseph E. Johnston's army, and then attack either Sherman or Grant before the two Union armies could combine.

But Lee's attack on Fort Stedman was a disaster, and when he evacuated Petersburg, Grant's army was close behind. Jefferson Davis and the Confederate government evacuated Richmond on April 2 and headed westward using the railroad. Davis would eventually get all the way to Georgia before being captured.

Lincoln was visiting General Grant near the front lines when Lee's Fort Stedman attack was launched. On April 4, Lincoln decided to visit Richmond. Taking a small escort with him, he walked through Richmond and went to Davis' former residence. "This must have been President Davis' chair," he said as he quietly sat down behind the desk of the Confederate chief.[41]

While walking through the city, hundreds of former slaves surrounded Lincoln, and many of them fell on their knees to express their thanks. Embarrassed, he told them that it was not right to thank him for their freedom, but they should instead thank God. Once, when an amused friend told Lincoln that he heard an old white-haired slave express a sense of awe about the president, claiming that "Massah Linkum, he eberywhar. He know eberyting. He walk de earf like de Lord!" Lincoln became silent. He got up from his chair, and silently paced the room. Finally he sat down and said impressively, "It is a momentous thing to be the instrument, under Providence, of the liberation of a race."[42]

Soon after his visit to Richmond, Lincoln returned to Washington to wait for Grant's reports about his pursuit of Lee. Lincoln finally received good news on April 9, when Grant sent a telegraph stating that Lee had surrendered his army. All that remained was the surrender of a few smaller armies, including those commanded by Joseph E. Johnston in North Carolina, Richard Taylor in Alabama, and E. Kirby Smith in the Trans-Mississippi Region.

On April 11, Lincoln made his last public speech. He spoke at length about the problems lying ahead with the reconstruction of the South and the establishment of suffrage for the black race. He expressed hope that the Southern states could be brought back into the Union soon, and announced that another proclamation of Thanksgiving would be forthcoming.

In the audience, listening to this speech, was the actor John Wilkes Booth. Angered by Lincoln's proposal for black voting rights, Booth vowed that this would be Lincoln's last speech. On the evening of April 14 he shot the president in the back of the head while Lincoln and his wife were watching a play at Ford's Theatre in Washington. Abraham Lincoln died the following morning at 7:22 a.m., and one by one, the church bells of Washington took up a mournful, steady peal.

Secretary of War Edwin Stanton, who with various cabinet members, friends, and family had sat up with the dying president, took a last look at his chief and said tremulously, "Now he belongs to the ages."[43]

Part II

Lincoln's Speeches and Writings

Chapter 2

Our Debt to the Nation's Founders

As a child, Lincoln had been taught to respect the authors of the Declaration of Independence and leaders such as Thomas Jefferson and George Washington. When he grew older and learned more about their vision for America, he frequently compared his generation's actions against what he perceived the founders expected. The following are a few of Lincoln's expressions of respect and gratitude to the founders of the government and authors of the Declaration of Independence.

This is an excerpt from a speech at the Young Men's Lyceum of Springfield, Illinois on January 27, 1838. Many regard it as Lincoln's first great speech, and in it he proclaimed his respect for the writers of the Declaration of Independence.

I do not mean to say that the scenes of the Revolution are now or ever will be entirely forgotten, but that, like everything else, they must fade upon the memory of the world, and grow more and more dim by the lapse of time. In history, we hope, they will be read of, and recounted, so long as the Bible shall be read; but even granting that they will, their influence cannot be what it heretofore has been. Even then they cannot be so universally known nor so vividly felt as they were by the generation just gone to rest. At the close of that struggle, nearly every adult male had been a participator in some of its scenes. The consequence was that of those scenes, in the form of a husband, a father, a son, or a brother, a living history was to be found in every family—a history bearing the indubitable testimonies of its own authenticity, in the limbs mangled, in the scars of wounds received, in the midst of the very scenes related—a history, too, that could be read and understood alike by all, the wise and the ignorant, the learned and the unlearned. But those histories are gone. They can be read no more forever. They were a fortress of strength; but what invading foeman could never do, the silent artillery of time has done—the leveling of its walls. They are gone. They were a forest of giant oaks; but the all restless hurricane has swept over them, and left only here and there a lonely trunk, despoiled of its verdure, shorn of its foliage, unshading and unshaded, to murmur in a few more gentle breezes, and to combat with its mutilated limbs a few more ruder storms, then to sink and be no more.

They were pillars of the temple of liberty; and now that they have crumbled away that temple must fall unless we, their descendants, supply their places with other pillars, hewn from the solid quarry of sober reason. Passion has helped us, but can do so no more. It will in future be our enemy. Reason—cold, calculating, unimpassioned reason—must furnish all the materials for our future support and defense. Let those materials be molded into general intelligence, sound morality, and, in particular, a reverence for the Constitution and laws; and that we improved to the last, that we remained free to the last, that we revered his name to the last, that during his long sleep we permitted no hostile foot to pass over or desecrate his resting place, shall be that which to learn the last trump shall awaken our Washington.

Upon these let the proud fabric of freedom rest, as the rock of its basis; and as truly as has been said of the only greater institution, "the gates of hell shall not prevail against it."[1]

Lincoln's love for the Declaration of Independence was probably one of the major reasons for his opposition to slavery. Below is a fragment of an 1854 speech, made before an audience in Peoria, Illinois, in which Lincoln proclaimed his respect for the Declaration, its authors, and their intention to limit slavery.

[N]o man is good enough to govern another man without that other's consent. I say this is the leading principle, the sheet-anchor of American republicanism. Our Declaration of Independence says:

"We hold these truths to be self-evident: That all men are created equal; that they are endowed by their Creator with certain inalienable rights; that among these are life, liberty, and the pursuit of happiness. That to secure these rights, governments are instituted among men, 'deriving their just powers from the consent of the governed.'

I have quoted so much at this time merely to show that, according to our ancient faith, the just powers of governments are derived from the consent of the governed. Now the relation of master and slave is pro tanto a total violation of this principle. The master not only governs the slave without his consent, but he governs him by a set of rules altogether different from those which he prescribes for himself. Allow all the governed an equal voice in the government, and that, and that only, is self-government . . .

. . . In support of his application of the doctrine of self-government, Senator Douglas has sought to bring to his aid the opinions and examples of our Revolutionary fathers. I am glad he has done this. I love the sentiments of those old-time men, and shall be most happy to abide by their opinions. He shows us that when it was in contemplation for the colonies to break off from Great Britain, and set up a new government for themselves, several of the States instructed their delegates to go for the measure, provided each State should be allowed to regulate its domestic concerns in its own way. I do not quote; but this in substance. This was right; I see nothing objectionable in it. I also think it probable that it had some reference to the existence of slavery among them. I will not deny that it had. But had it any reference to the carrying of slavery into new countries? That is the question, and we will let the fathers themselves answer it.

This same generation of men, and mostly the same individuals of the generation who declared this principle, who declared independence, who fought the war of the Revolution through, who afterward made the Constitution under which we still live—these same men passed the ordinance of '87, declaring that slavery should never go to the Northwest Territory. I have no doubt Judge Douglas thinks they were very inconsistent in this. It is a question of discrimination between them and him. But there is not an inch of ground left for his claiming that their opinions, their example, their authority, are on his side in the controversy.[2]

In an 1857 speech in Springfield, Lincoln attacked the positions that the chief justice of the Supreme Court, Roger Taney, and Stephen A. Douglas, his future rival for the U.S. Senate, took on the status of African Americans. Taney had recently handed down the decision on Dred Scott, a slave that sued for his freedom.

In the Dred Scott Decision, Taney stated that black people had no legal rights because they were not citizens of the United States. Stephen A. Douglas, perhaps the most influential Democratic senator in the United States, declared that the Declaration of Independence was never intended to include black people, but that it was written exclusively for the white race. The following argument is typical of Lincoln's use of the Declaration to attack an opponent's position.

Chief Justice Taney, in his opinion in the Dred Scott case, admits that the language of the Declaration is broad enough to include the whole human family, but he and Judge Douglas argue that the authors of that instrument did not intend to include African-Americans, by the fact that they did not at once actually place them on an equality with the whites. Now this grave argument comes to just nothing at all, by the other fact that they did not at once, or ever afterward, actually place all white people on an equality with one another. And this is the staple argument of both the chief justice and the senator for doing this obvious violence to the plain, unmistakable language of the Declaration.

I think the authors of that notable instrument intended to include all men, but they did not intend to declare all men equal in all respects. They did not mean to say all were equal in color, size, intellect, moral develop-ments, or social capacity. They defined with tolerable distinctness in what respects they did consider all men created equal—equal with "certain in-alienable rights, among which are life, liberty, and the pursuit of happi-ness." This they said, and this they meant. They did not mean to assert the obvious untruth that all were then actually enjoying that equality, nor yet that they were about to confer it immediately upon them. In fact, they had no power to confer such a boon. They meant simply to declare the right, so that enforcement of it might follow as fast as circumstances should permit.

They meant to set up a standard maxim for free society, which should be familiar to all, and revered by all; constantly looked to, constantly la-bored for, and even though never perfectly attained, constantly approxi-mated, and thereby constantly spreading and deepening its influence and augmenting the happiness and value of life to all people of all colors every-where. The assertion that "all men are created equal" was of no practical use in effecting our separation from Great Britain; and it was placed in the Declaration not for that, but for future use. Its authors meant it to be—as, thank God, it is now proving itself—a tumbling-block to all those who in after times might seek to turn a free people back into the hateful paths of despotism. They knew the proneness of prosperity to breed tyrants, and they meant when such should reappear in this fair land and commence their vocation, they should find left for them at least one hard nut to crack.

I have now briefly expressed my view of the meaning and object of that part of the Declaration of Independence which declares that "all men are created equal."[3]

In Chicago on July 10, 1858, Lincoln spoke before a large crowd. In it he refuted what Senator Douglas had said the previous evening and prepared himself for the debate appointments that were about to follow.

Now, it happens that we meet together once every year, somewhere about the 4th of July, for some reason or other. These 4th of July gatherings I suppose have their uses. If you will indulge me, I will state what I sup-pose to be some of them.

We are now a mighty nation: we are thirty, or about thirty, millions of people, and we own and inhabit about one fifteenth part of the dry land of the whole earth. We run our memory back over the pages of history for about eighty-two years, and we discover that we were then a very small people, in point of numbers vastly inferior to what we are now, with a vastly less extent of country, with vastly less of everything we deem desir-able among men. We look upon the change as exceedingly advantageous to us and to our posterity, and we fix upon something that happened away back as in some way or other being connected with this rise of prosperity.

We find a race of men living in that day whom we claim as our fathers and grandfathers; they were iron men; they fought for the principle that they were contending for; and we understood that by what they then did it has followed that the degree of prosperity which we now enjoy has come to us. We hold this annual celebration to remind ourselves of all the good done in this process of time, of how it was done and who did it, and how we are historically connected with it; and we go from these meetings in better humor with ourselves—we feel more attached the one to the other, and more firmly bound to the country we inhabit. In every way we are better men, in the age, and race, and country in which we live, for these celebrations. But after we have done all this, we have not yet reached the whole. There is something else connected with it. We have, besides these men—descended blood from our ancestors—among us, perhaps half our people who are not descendants at all of these men; they are men who have come from Europe,—German, Irish, French, and Scandinavian,—men that have come from Europe themselves, or whose ancestors have come hither and settled here, finding themselves our equal in all things. If they look back through this history to trace their connection with those days by blood, they find they have none; they cannot carry themselves back into that glorious epoch and make themselves feel that they are part of us; but when they look through that old Declaration of Independence, they find that those old men say that "We hold these truths to be self-evident, that all men are created equal," and then they feel that that moral sentiment taught in that day evidences their relation to those men, that it is the father of all moral principle in them, and that they have a right to claim it as though they were blood of the blood, and flesh of the flesh, of the men who wrote that Declaration, and so they are. That is the electric cord in that Declaration that links the hearts of patriotic and liberty-loving men together, that will link those patriotic hearts as long as the love of freedom exists in the minds of men throughout the world.[4]

In Lewistown, Illinois on August 17, 1858, Lincoln entreated his audience to come back to the Declaration of Independence.

The Declaration of Independence was formed by the representatives of American liberty from thirteen States of the Confederacy, twelve of which were slave-holding communities. We need not discuss the way or the reason of their becoming slave-holding communities. It is sufficient for our purpose that all of them greatly deplored the evil and that they placed a provision in the Constitution which they supposed would gradually remove the disease by cutting off its source. This was the abolition of the slave trade. So general was the conviction, the public determination, to abolish the African slave trade, that the provision which I have referred to as being placed in the Constitution declared that it should not be abolished prior to the year 1808. A constitutional provision was necessary to prevent the people, through Congress, from putting a stop to the traffic immediately at the close of the war. Now if slavery had been a good thing, would the fathers of the republic have taken a step calculated to diminish its beneficent influences among themselves, and snatch the boon wholly from their posterity? These communities, by their representatives in old Independence Hall, said to the whole world of men: "We hold these truths to be self-evident: that all men are created equal; that they are endowed by their Creator with certain inalienable rights; that among these are life, liberty, and the pursuit of happiness." This was their majestic interpretation of the economy of the Universe. This was their lofty, and wise, and noble understanding of the justice of the Creator to his creatures. Yes, gentlemen, to all his creatures, to the whole great family of man. In their enlightened belief, nothing stamped with the Divine image and likeness was sent into the world to be trodden on and degraded and imbruted by its fellows. They grasped not only the whole race of man then living, but they reached forward and seized upon the farthest posterity. They erected a beacon to guide their children, and their children's children, and the countless myriads who should inhabit the earth in other ages.

Wise statesmen as they were, they knew the tendency of prosperity to breed tyrants, and so they established these great self-evident truths, that when in the distant future some man, some faction, some interest, should set up the doctrine that none but rich men, or none but white men, or none but Anglo-Saxon white men, were entitled to life, liberty, and the pursuit of happiness, their posterity might look up again to the Declaration of Independence and take courage to renew the battle which their fathers began, so that truth and justice and mercy and all the humane and Christian virtues might not be extinguished from the land; so that no man would hereafter dare to limit and circumscribe the great principles on which the temple of liberty was being built.

Now, my countrymen, if you have been taught doctrines conflicting with the great landmarks of the Declaration of Independence; if you have listened to suggestions which would take away from its grandeur and mutilate the fair symmetry of its proportions; if you have been inclined to believe that all men are not created equal in those inalienable rights enumerated by our chart of liberty, let me entreat you to come back. Return to the fountain whose waters spring close by the blood of the revolution. Think nothing of me—take no thought for the political fate of any man whomsoever but come back to the truths that are in the Declaration of Independence. You may do anything with me you choose, if you will but heed these sacred principles. You may not only defeat me for the Senate, but you may take me and put me to death. While pretending no indifference to earthly honors, I do claim to be actuated in this contest by something higher than an anxiety for office. I charge you to drop every paltry and insignificant thought for any man's success. It is nothing; I am nothing; Judge Douglas is nothing. But do not destroy that immortal emblem of Humanity—the Declaration of American Independence.[5]

In the last of the Lincoln-Douglas Debates at Alton, Illinois, Lincoln emphasized the argument between the right and wrong of slavery. He closed with an analogy that was intended to leave the audience with a lasting impression of the timeless importance of their debates over this issue.

I have stated upon former occasions, and I may as well state again, what I understand to be the real issue in this controversy between Judge Douglas and myself. On the point of my wanting to make war between the free and the slave States, there has been no issue between us. So, too, when he assumes that I am in favor of introducing a perfect social and political equality between the white and black races. These are false issues, upon which Judge Douglas has tried to force the controversy. There is no foundation in truth for the charge that I maintain either of these propositions. The real issue in this controversy—the one pressing upon every mind—is the sentiment on the part of one class that looks upon the institution of slavery as a wrong, and of another class that does not look upon it as a wrong. The sentiment that contemplates the institution of slavery in this country as a wrong is the sentiment of the Republican party. It is the sentiment around which all their actions, all their arguments circle; from which all their propositions radiate. They look upon it as being a moral, social and political wrong; and while they contemplate it as such, they nevertheless have due regard for its actual existence among us, and the difficulties of getting rid of it in any satisfactory way and to all the constitutional obligations thrown about it. Yet having a due regard for these, they desire a policy in regard to it that looks to its not creating any more danger. They insist that it should as far as may be, be treated as a wrong, and one of the methods of treating it as a wrong is to make provision that it shall grow no larger. . . .

On this subject of treating it as a wrong, and limiting its spread, let me say a word. Has any thing ever threatened the existence of this Union save and except this very institution of slavery? What is it that we hold most dear amongst us? Our own liberty and prosperity. What has ever threatened our liberty and prosperity save and except this institution of slavery? If this is true, how do you propose to improve the condition of things by enlarging slavery—by spreading it out and making it bigger? You may have a wen or a cancer upon your person and not be able to cut it out lest you bleed to death; but surely it is no way to cure it, to engraft it and spread it over your whole body. That is no proper way of treating what you regard a wrong. You see this peaceful way of dealing with it as a wrong—restricting the spread of it, and not allowing it to go into new countries where it has not already existed. That is the peaceful way, the old-fashioned way, the way in which the fathers themselves set us the example. . . .

[This] is the issue that will continue in this country when these poor tongues of Judge Douglas and myself shall be silent. It is the eternal struggle between these two principles—right and wrong—throughout the world. They are the two principles that have stood face to face from the beginning of time; and will ever continue to struggle. The one is the common right of humanity, and the other the divine right of kings. It is the same principle in whatever shape it develops itself. It is the same spirit that says, "You toil and work and earn bread, and I'll eat it." No matter in what shape it comes, whether from the mouth of a king who seeks to bestride the people of his own nation and live by the fruit of their labor, or from one race of men as an apology for enslaving another race, it is the same tyrannical principle.[6]

At Independence Hall in Philadelphia on February 22, 1861, president-elect Abraham Lincoln eloquently communicated his belief that the principles of the Declaration of Independence belong to all men, for all time.

I have never had a feeling, politically, that did not spring from the sentiments embodied in the Declaration of Independence. I have often pondered over the dangers which were incurred by the men who assembled here and framed and adopted that Declaration. I have pondered over the toils that were endured by the officers and soldiers of the army who achieved that independence. I have often inquired of myself what great principle or idea it was that kept this Confederacy so long together. It was not the mere matter of separation of the colonies from the motherland, but that sentiment in the Declaration of Independence which gave liberty not alone to the people of this country, but hope to all the world, for all future time. It was that which gave promise that in due time the weights would be lifted from the shoulders of all men, and that all should have an equal chance. This is the sentiment embodied in the Declaration of Independence.

Now, my friends, can this country be saved on that basis? If it can, I will consider myself one of the happiest men in the world if I can help save it. If it cannot be saved upon that principle, it will be truly awful. But if this country cannot be saved without giving up that principle, I was about to say I would rather be assassinated on this spot than surrender it.[7]

In these notes, written sometime before his First Inaugural Address, Lincoln was continuing to formulate his ideas on the relationship between the Declaration of Independence, the Constitution, and the Union.

All this is not the result of accident. It has a philosophical cause. Without the Constitution and the Union, we could not have attained the result; but even these, are not the primary cause of our great prosperity. There is something back of these, entwining itself more closely about the human heart. That something, is the principle of "Liberty to all"—the principle that clears the path for all—gives hope to all—and, by consequence, enterprize, and industry to all.

The expression of that principle, in our Declaration of Independence, was most happy, and fortunate. Without this, as well as with it, we could have declared our independence of Great Britain; but without it, we could not, I think, have secured our free government, and consequent prosperity. No oppressed people will fight, and endure, as our fathers did, without the promise of something better, than a mere change of masters.

The assertion of that principle, at that time, was the word, "fitly spoken" which has proved an "apple of gold" to us. The Union, and the Constitution, are the picture of silver, subsequently framed around it. The picture was made, not to conceal, or destroy the apple; but to adorn, and preserve it. The picture was made for the apple—not the apple for the picture.

So let us act, that neither picture, nor apple shall ever be blurred, or bruised or broken.

That we may so act, we must study, and understand the points of danger.[8]

Chapter 3

The People

While growing up among pioneers in the Midwestern wilderness, Lincoln developed a life-long respect for the character and resourcefulness of the American people. He considered them the most intelligent, industrious, and resourceful people on Earth. He said that as long as they retained "their virtue and vigilance" they could never be successfully misled by any corrupt political leader. The following speeches and writings, most of which are taken from the 1850s and 1860s, illustrate Lincoln's faith in the people.

Early in his political career Lincoln voiced his confidence in the people.

The people know their rights, and they are never slow to assert and maintain them, when they are invaded.[1]

In this excerpt from his 1838 Lyceum Address, Lincoln praised the American people and warned them of future danger.

In the great journal of things happening under the sun, we, the American People, find our account running, under date of the nineteenth century of the Christian era. We find ourselves in the peaceful possession, of the fairest portion of the earth, as regards extent of territory, fertility of soil, and salubrity of climate. We find ourselves under the government of a system of political institutions conducing more essentially to the ends of civil and religious liberty than any of which the history of former times tells us. We, when mounting the stage of existence, found ourselves the legal inheritors of these fundamental blessings. We toiled not in the acquirement or establishment of them; they are a legacy bequeathed us, by a once hardy, brave, and patriotic, but now lamented and departed race of ancestors. Theirs was the task (and nobly they performed it) to possess themselves, and through themselves, us, of this goodly land; and to uprear upon its hills and its valleys, a political edifice of liberty and equal rights; 'tis ours only, to transmit these, the former, unprofaned by the foot of an invader; the latter, undecayed by the lapse of time, and untorn by usurpation—to the latest generation that fate shall permit the world to know. This task of gratitude to our fathers, justice to ourselves, duty to posterity, and love for our species in general, all imperatively require us faithfully to perform.

How, then, shall we perform it? At what point shall we expect the approach of danger? By what means shall we fortify against it? Shall we expect some transatlantic military giant, to step the Ocean, and crush us at a blow? Never! All the armies of Europe, Asia and Africa combined, with all the treasure of the earth (our own excepted) in their military chest; with a Bonaparte for a commander, could not by force, take a drink from the Ohio, or make a track on the Blue Ridge in a trial of a thousand years.

At what point then is the approach of danger to be expected? I answer, if it ever reach us, it must spring up amongst us. It cannot come from abroad. If destruction be our lot, we must ourselves be its author and finisher. As a nation of freemen, we must live through all time, or die by suicide. . . .

I know the American People are much attached to their government; I know they would suffer much for its sake; I know they would endure evils long and patiently, before they would ever think of exchanging it for another. Yet, notwithstanding all this, if the laws be continually despised and disregarded, if their rights to be secure in their persons and property, are held by no better tenure than the caprice of a mob, the alienation of their affections from the Government is the natural consequence; and to that, sooner or later, it must come.

Here, then, is one point at which danger may be expected.

The question recurs "how shall we fortify against it?" The answer is simple. Let every American, every lover of liberty, every well wisher to his posterity, swear by the blood of the Revolution, never to violate in the least particular, the laws of the country; and never to tolerate their violation by others. As the patriots of seventy-six did to the support of the Declaration of Independence, so to the support of the Constitution and Laws, let every American pledge his life, his property, and his sacred honor; let every man remember that to violate the law, is to trample on the blood of his father, and to tear the charter of his own, and his children's liberty. Let reverence for the laws be breathed by every American mother, to the lisping babe, that prattles on her lap; let it be taught in schools, in seminaries, and in colleges; let it be written in primmers, spelling books, and in Almanacs; let it be preached from the pulpit, proclaimed in legislative halls, and enforced in courts of justice. And, in short, let it become the political religion of the nation; and let the old and the young, the rich and the poor, the grave and the gay, of all sexes and tongues, and colors and conditions, sacrifice unceasingly upon its altars.

While ever a state of feeling, such as this, shall universally, or even, very generally prevail throughout the nation, vain will be every effort, and fruitless every attempt, to subvert our national freedom.[2]

Lincoln believed the people were the masters of their government.

The people of these United States are the rightful masters of both congresses and courts not to overthrow the Constitution, but to overthrow the men who pervert the Constitution.[3]

Lincoln used a simple anecdote to illustrate the character of the people.

I think very much of the people, as an old friend said he thought of woman. He said when he lost his first wife, who had been a great help to him in his business, he thought he was ruined—that he could never find another to fill her place. At length, however, he married another, who he found did quite as well as the first, and that his opinion now was that any woman would do well who was well done by. So I think of the whole people of this nation—they will ever do well if well done by. We will try to do well by them in all parts of the country, North and South, with entire confidence that all will be well with all of us.[4]

In the following excerpt from a speech in Ohio, president-elect Lincoln expressed confidence in both the people and God.

It is true . . . that very great responsibility rests upon me in the position to which the votes of the American people have called me. I am deeply sensible of that weighty responsibility. . . . I turn, then, and look to the American people, and to that God who has never forsaken them.[5]

Lincoln spoke to citizens of Indiana and reminded them that it would be the people's responsibility to maintain the Union.

In all the trying positions in which I shall be placed, and doubtless I shall be placed in many trying ones, my reliance will be placed upon you and the people of the United States—and I wish you to remember now and forever, that it is your business, and not mine; that if the union of these States, and the liberties of this people, shall be lost, it is but little to any one man of fifty-two years of age, but a great deal to the thirty millions of people who inhabit these United States, and to their posterity in all coming time. It is your business to rise up and preserve the Union and liberty, for yourselves, and not for me. I desire they shall be constitutionally preserved.

I, as already intimated, am but an accidental instrument, temporary, and to serve but for a limited time, but I appeal to you again to constantly bear in mind that with you, and not with politicians, not with Presidents, not with office-seekers, but with you, is the question, "Shall the Union and shall the liberties of this country be preserved to the latest generation?"[6]

In Albany, New York, Lincoln again revealed his confidence in the people and God.

In the mean time, if we have patience, if we restrain ourselves, if we allow ourselves not to run off in a passion, I still have confidence that the Almighty, the Maker of the universe, will, through the instrumentality of this great and intelligent people, bring us through this as he has through all the other difficulties of our country. Relying on this, I again thank you for this generous reception.[7]

In Poughkeepsie, New York, Lincoln boasted of the character and fortunes of the American people.

It is with your aid, as the people, that I think we shall be able to preserve—not the country, for the country will preserve itself, but the institutions of the country; those institutions which have made us free, intelligent and happy—the most free, the most intelligent and the happiest people on the globe.[8]

Shortly before being inaugurated president, Lincoln stated he would rely on the strength of "the masses" to sustain him.

I feel that, under God, in the strength of the arms and wisdom of the heads of these masses, after all, must be my support. As I have often had occasion to say, I repeat to you—I am quite sure I do not deceive myself when I tell you I bring to the work an honest heart; I dare not tell you that I bring a head sufficient for it. If my own strength should fail, I shall at least fall back upon these masses, who, I think, under any circumstances will not fail.[9]

In this excerpt from Lincoln's first inaugural address, Lincoln expressed the opinion that the people are worthy to be trusted and would live up to future challenges.

Why should there not be a patient confidence in the ultimate justice of the people? Is there any better, or equal hope, in the world? In our present differences, is either party without faith of being in the right? If the Almighty

Ruler of nations, with his eternal truth and justice, be on your side of the North, or on yours of the South, that truth, and that justice, will surely prevail, by the judgment of this great tribunal, the American people.

By the frame of the government under which we live, this same people have wisely given their public servants but little power for mischief; and have, with equal wisdom, provided for the return of that little to their own hands at very short intervals.

While the people retain their virtue, and vigilence, no administration, by any extreme of wickedness or folly, can very seriously injure the government, in the short space of four years.[10]

Lincoln declared his confidence in the people first, and then the government.

In a word, the people will save their government, if the government itself will do its part, only indifferently well.[11]

A few months after the Civil War began, Lincoln called Congress into special session on July 4, 1861. In this, his first address to Congress, he displayed his confidence the people would triumph.

This is essentially a People's contest. On the side of the Union, it is a struggle for maintaining in the world, that form, and substance of government, whose leading object is, to elevate the condition of men—to lift artificial weights from all shoulders—to clear the paths of laudable pursuit for all—to afford all, an unfettered start, and a fair chance, in the race of life. Yielding to partial, and temporary departures, from necessity, this is the leading object of the government for whose existence we contend.

I am most happy to believe that the plain people understand, and appreciate this. It is worthy of note, that while in this, the government's hour of trial, large numbers of those in the Army and Navy, who have been favored with the offices, have resigned, and proved false to the hand which had pampered them, not one common soldier, or common sailor is known to have deserted his flag.[12]

In this excerpt from a letter to the Workingmen of Manchester, England, Lincoln expressed his belief that although the American people had great advantages, they also had great responsibilities.

The resources, advantages, and powers of the American people are very great, and they have, consequently, succeeded to equally great responsibilities. It seems to have devolved upon them to test whether a government established on the principles of human freedom can be maintained against an effort to build one upon the exclusive foundation of human bondage.[13]

Chapter 4

Government and Economy

Lincoln believed that democracy was the best form of government ever devised by man. He also supported the American system of labor, because it gave even the most humble the opportunity to improve themselves. The following speeches and writings illustrate Lincoln's increasing understanding of the significance of democratic government. The first writings manifest the mind of a young candidate that is concerned with little more than getting elected and providing his constituents with basic civic improvements. The last manifest a leader that in dealing with monumental problems appreciates the significance of democratic government perhaps better than anyone else.

While in the state legislature, Lincoln demonstrated his belief that the person that molds public sentiment is more important than those that simply pass laws.

In this and like communities, public sentiment is everything. With public sentiment, nothing can fail; without it, nothing can succeed. Consequently he who molds public sentiment goes deeper than he who enacts statutes or pronounces decisions. He makes statutes and decisions possible or impossible to be executed.[1]

In this excerpt from a letter to a Democrat from Bond County, Illinois, Lincoln defended increased taxation. At the close of the letter he pointed out that even if the wealthy objected to it, they were too few in number to prevent the proposed law's passage.

The only question is as to sustaining the change before the people. I believe it can be sustained, because it does not increase the tax upon the "many poor" but upon the "wealthy few" by taxing the land that is worth $50 or $100 per acre, in proportion to its value, instead of, as heretofore, no

51

more than that which was worth but $5 per acre. This valuable land, as is well known, belongs, not to the poor, but to the wealthy citizen.

On the other hand, the wealthy can not justly complain, because the change is equitable within itself, and also a sine qua non to a compliance with the Constitution. If, however, the wealthy should, regardless of the justness of the complaint, as men often are, when interest is involved in the question, complain of the change, it is still to be remembered, that they are not sufficiently numerous to carry the elections.[2]

During a speech made in the state legislature on the subject of the national bank, Lincoln showed some signs of the facility with words he would one day become famous for.

Many free countries have lost their liberty, and ours may lose hers; but if she shall, be it my proudest plume, not that I was the last to desert, but that I never deserted her. I know that the great volcano at Washington, aroused and directed by the evil spirit that reigns there, is belching forth the lava of political corruption, in a current broad and deep, which is sweeping with frightful velocity over the whole length and breadth of the land, bidding fair to leave unscathed no green spot or living thing, while on its bosom are riding, like demons on the waves of hell, the imps of that evil spirit, and fiendishly taunting all those who dare resist its destroying course, with the hopelessness of their effort; and knowing this, I cannot deny that all may be swept away. Broken by it, I, too, may be; bow to it I never will. The probability that we may fall in the struggle ought not to deter us from the support of a cause we believe to be just; it shall not deter me. If ever I feel the soul within me elevate and expand to those dimensions not wholly unworthy of its almighty Architect, it is when I contemplate the cause of my country, deserted by all the world beside, and I standing up boldly and alone and hurling defiance at her victorious oppressors. Here, without contemplating consequences, before high heaven, and in the face of the world, I swear eternal fidelity to the just cause, as I deem it, of the land of my life, my liberty and my love. And who, that thinks with me, will not fearlessly adopt the oath that I take. Let none faulter, who thinks he is right, and we may succeed. But, if after all, we shall fail, be it so. We still shall have the proud consolation of saying to our consciences, and to the departed shade of our country's freedom, that the cause approved of our judgment, and adored of our hearts, in disaster, in chains, in torture, in death, we never faultered in defending.[3]

In this excerpt from an early 1848 speech in Congress, Lincoln supported people that wished to discard their existing government and form a new one. These words would haunt him 20 years later, when he confronted the Southern states that wanted to do precisely that.

Any people anywhere, being inclined and having the power, have the right to rise up, and shake off the existing government, and form a new one that suits them better. This is a most valuable, a most sacred right—a right, which we hope and believe, is to liberate the world. Nor is this right confined to cases in which the whole people of an existing government may choose to exercise it. Any portion of such people that can, may revolutionize, and make their own, of so much of the teritory as they inhabit. More than this, a majority of any portion of such people may revolutionize, putting down a minority, intermingled with, or near about them, who may oppose their movement. Such minority, was precisely the case, of the tories of our own revolution.[4]

While in Congress, Lincoln succinctly stated his practical outlook on government policy and politics.

The true rule, in determining to embrace, or reject any thing, is not whether it have any evil in it; but whether it have more of evil, than of good. There are few things wholly evil, or wholly good. Almost every thing, especially of governmental policy, is an inseparable compound of the two; so that our best judgment of the preponderance between them is continually demanded.[5]

In a letter to his lazy stepbrother, replying to a repeated request for a handout, Lincoln encouraged him to go to work. Hoping to change his relative's idle ways, he offered to pay him a dollar for every dollar he earned on his own.

Dear Johnston:

Your request for eighty dollars I do not think it best to comply with now. At the various times when I have helped you a little you have said to me "We can get along very well now;" but in a very short time I find you in the same difficulty again. Now, this can only happen by some defect in your conduct. What that defect is, I think I know. You are not lazy, and still you are an idler. I doubt whether, since I saw you, you have done a good whole day's work in any one day. You do not very much dislike to work; and still you do not work much, merely because it does not seem to you that you could get much for it. This habit of uselessly wasting time, is the whole difficulty; it is vastly important to you, and still more so to your children, that you should break the habit. It is more important to them, because they have longer to live, and can keep out of an idle habit before they are in it; easier than they can get out after they are in.

You are now in need of some money; and what I propose is, that you shall go to work, "tooth and nail" for some body who will give you money for it. Let father and your boys take charge of things at home, prepare for a crop, and make the crop; and you go to work for the best money wages, or in discharge of any debt you owe, that you can get; and to secure you a fair reward for your labor, I now promise you, that for every dollar you will, between this and the first of next May, get for your own labor, either in money, or in your own indebtedness, I will then give you one other dollar. By this, if you hire yourself at ten dollars a month, from me you will get ten more, making twenty dollars a month for your work. In this, I do not mean you shall go off to St. Louis, or the lead mines, or the gold mines, in California, but I mean for you to go at it for the best wages you can get close to home in Coles county. Now if you will do this, you will soon be out of debt, and what is better, you will have a habit that will keep you from getting in debt again. But if I should now clear you out of debt, next year you will be just as deep in as ever. You say you would almost give your place in Heaven for seventy or eighty dollars. Then you value your place in heaven very cheap for I am sure you can, with the offer I make, get the seventy or eighty dollars for four or five months work. You say if I furnish you the money you will deed me the land, and, if you dont pay the money back, you will deliver possession. Nonsense! If you can't now live with the land, how will you then live without it? You have always been kind to me, and I do not now mean to be unkind to you. On the contrary, if you will but follow my advice, you will find it worth more than eight times eighty dollars to you.[6]

In 1854, Lincoln expressed his belief that the government's power should be limited.

The legitimate object of government is to do for a community of people whatever they need to have done, but can not do, at all, or can not, so well do, for themselves—in their separate, and individual capacities.

In all that the people can individually do as well for themselves, government ought not to interfere. The desirable things which the individuals of a people can not do, or can not well do, for themselves, fall into two classes: those which have relation to wrongs, and those which have not. Each of these branch off into an infinite variety of subdivisions.

The first—that in relation to wrongs—embraces all crimes, misdemeanors, and non-performance of contracts. The other embraces all which, in its nature, and without wrong, requires combined action, as public roads and highways, public schools, charities, pauperism, orphanage, estates of the deceased, and the machinery of government itself.

From this it appears that if all men were just, there still would be some, though not so much, need of government.[7]

In this fragment, written sometime in mid-1854, Lincoln succinctly stated his confidence in American government.

Most governments have been based, practically, on the denial of equal rights of men, as I have, in part, stated them; ours began, by affirming those rights. They said, some men are too ignorant and vicious to share in government. Possibly so, said we; and, by your system, you would always keep them ignorant and vicious. We proposed to give all a chance; and we expected the weak to grow stronger, the ignorant, wiser; and all better, and happier together.

We made the experiment; and the fruit is before us. Look at it, think of it. Look at it, in its aggregate grandeur, of extent of country, and numbers of population—of ship, and steamboat, and rail.[8]

In late 1857 Lincoln demonstrated his belief that the ballot box was more powerful than the threat of war.

To give the victory to the right, not bloody bullets, but peaceful ballots only, are necessary. Thanks to our good old constitution, and organization under it, these alone are necessary. It only needs that every right thinking man shall go to the polls, and without fear or prejudice, vote as he thinks.[9]

Lincoln never forgot where the true power of democratic government came from.

Our government rests in public opinion. Whoever can change public opinion can change the government.[10]

In 1858 Lincoln provided this succinct definition of democracy.

As I would not be a slave, so I would not be a master. This expresses my idea of democracy. Whatever differs from this, to the extent of the difference, is no democracy.[11]

When speaking to the Wisconsin Agricultural Society, Lincoln praised the economic system that allowed the penniless beginner to work his way up to eventual prosperity. He probably had his own life in mind as a prime example of this.

The prudent, penniless beginner in the world, labors for wages awhile, saves a surplus with which to buy tools or land, for himself; then labors on his own account another while, and at length hires another new beginner to help him. This, say its advocates, is free labor—the just and generous, and prosperous system, which opens the way for all—gives hope to all, and energy, and progress, and improvement of condition to all. If any continue through life in the condition of the hired laborer, it is not the fault of the system, but because of either a dependent nature which prefers it, or improvidence, folly, or singular misfortune.[12]

In New Haven, Connecticut, Lincoln spoke out in favor of striking shoe workers, illustrating his belief in a system of labor that allowed employees to stop working if not satisfied with their conditions. He could not resist interjecting his belief that black men should be given the same right.

I am glad to see that a system of labor prevails in New England under which laborers CAN strike when they want to, where they are not obliged to work under all circumstances, and are not tied down and obliged to labor whether you pay them or not! I like the system which lets a man quit when he wants to, and wish it might prevail everywhere. One of the reasons why I am opposed to Slavery is just here. What is the true condition of the laborer? I take it that it is best for all to leave each man free to acquire property as fast as he can. Some will get wealthy. I don't believe in a law to prevent a man from getting rich; it would do more harm than good. So while we do not propose any war upon capital, we do wish to allow the humblest man an equal chance to get rich with everybody else. When one starts poor, as most do in the race of life, free society is such that he knows he can better his condition; he knows that there is no fixed condition of labor, for his whole life. I am not ashamed to confess that twenty five years ago I was a hired laborer, mauling rails, at work on a flat-boat—just what might happen to any poor man's son! I want every man to have the chance—and I believe a black man is entitled to it—in which he can better his condition—when he may look forward and hope to be a hired laborer this year and the next, work for himself afterward, and finally to hire men to work for him! That is the true system.[13]

Three months after he was elected president, Lincoln boarded the train that would take him from Springfield, Illinois to Washington, D.C. Along the way the train stopped at countless towns and cities in order to allow people to see their future leader. In Trenton, he spoke briefly to the state senate, and in a few sentences emphasized his respect for the writers of the Declaration of Independence, his faith in God, his commitment to democratic government, and his respect for the American people, whom he called God's "almost chosen."

Mr. President and Gentlemen of the Senate of the State of New Jersey: I am very grateful to you for the honorable reception of which I have been the object. I cannot but remember the place that New-Jersey holds in our early history. In the early Revolutionary struggle, few of the States among the old Thirteen had more of the battle-fields of the country within their limits than old New-Jersey. May I be pardoned if, upon this occasion, I mention that away back in my childhood, the earliest days of my being able to read, I got hold of a small book, such a one as few of the younger members have ever seen, Weem's "Life of Washington." I remember all the accounts there given of the battle fields and struggles for the liberties of the country, and none fixed themselves upon my imagination so deeply as the struggle here at Trenton, New-Jersey. The crossing of the river; the contest with the Hessians; the great hardships endured at that time, all fixed themselves on my memory more than any single Revolutionary event; and you all know, for you have all been boys, how these early impressions last longer than any others. I recollect thinking then, boy even though I was, that there must have been something more than common that those men struggled for. I am exceedingly anxious that that thing which they struggled for; that something even more than national independence; that something that held out a great promise to all the people of the world to all time to come; I am exceedingly anxious that this Union, the Constitution, and the liberties of the people shall be perpetuated in accordance with the original idea for which that struggle was made, and I shall be most happy indeed if I shall be an humble instrument in the hands of the Almighty, and of this, his almost chosen people, for perpetuating the object of that great struggle. You give me this reception, as I understand, without distinction of party. I learn that this body is composed of a majority of gentlemen who, in the exercise of their best judgment in the choice of a chief magistrate, did not think I was the man. I understand, nevertheless, that they came forward here to greet me as the constitutional President of the United States—as citizens of the United States, to meet the man who, for the time being, is the representative man of the nation, united by a purpose to perpetuate the Union and liberties of the people. As such, I accept this reception more gratefully than I could do did I believe it was tendered to me as an individual.[14]

In the following excerpt of Lincoln's First Inaugural Address, he attempted to explain the legal reasons why the Union must be preserved, and personally expressed his confidence that it would endure. He also stated that the "Union is older than the Constitution," which may have been a hint that the documents that preceded it (especially the Declaration of Independence) would receive equal or better treatment from the new president.

I hold, that in contemplation of universal law, and of the Constitution, the Union of these States is perpetual. Perpetuity is implied, if not expressed, in the fundamental law of all national governments. It is safe to assert that no government proper ever had a provision in its organic law for its own termination.

Continue to execute all the express provisions of our National Constitution, and the Union will endure forever—it being impossible to destroy it, except by some action not provided for in the instrument itself.

Again, if the United States be not a government proper, but an association of States in the nature of contract merely, can it, as a contract, be peaceably unmade, by less than all the parties who made it? One party to a contract may violate it—break it, so to speak; but does it not require all to lawfully rescind it?

Descending from these general principles, we find the proposition that, in legal contemplation, the Union is perpetual, confirmed by the history of the Union itself. The Union is much older than the Constitution. It was formed, in fact, by the Articles of Association in 1774. It was matured and continued by the Declaration of Independence in 1776. It was further matured and the faith of all the then thirteen States expressly plighted and engaged that it should be perpetual, by the Articles of Confederation in 1778. And finally, in 1787, one of the declared objects for ordaining and establishing the Constitution was "to form a more perfect union."

But if destruction of the Union, by one, or by a part only, of the States, be lawfully possible, the Union is less perfect than before the Constitution, having lost the vital element of perpetuity.

It follows from these views that no State, upon its own mere motion, can lawfully get out of the Union, that resolves and ordinances to that effect are legally void; and that acts of violence, within any State or States, against the authority of the United States, are insurrectionary or revolutionary, according to circumstances.

I therefore consider that, in view of the Constitution and the laws, the Union is unbroken; and, to the extent of my ability, I shall take care, as the Constitution itself expressly enjoins upon me, that the laws of the Union be faithfully executed in all the States. Doing this I deem to be only a simple duty on my part; and I shall perform it, so far as practicable, unless my rightful masters, the American people, shall withhold the requisite means, or, in some authoritative manner, direct the contrary. I trust this will not be regarded as a menace, but only as the declared purpose of the Union that it will constitutionally defend, and maintain itself.[15]

In his first annual message to Congress in December 1861, Lincoln emphasized the importance of setting up an expeditious means for citizens to process claims against the government during the war.

It is as much the duty of government to render prompt justice against itself, in favor of citizens, as it is to administer the same, between private individuals.[16]

---

*In the following fragment from a reply to the Presbyterian Church's General As-
sembly in mid-1863, Lincoln stated both his commitment to American government and dependence on God.*

As a pilot I have used my best exertions to keep afloat our Ship of
State, and shall be glad to resign my trust at the appointed time to another
pilot more skillful and successful than I may prove. In every case and at all
hazards the government must be perpetuated. Relying, as I do, upon the
Almighty Power, and encouraged as I am by these resolutions which you
have just read, with the support which I receive from Christian men, I shall
not hesitate to use all the means at my control to secure the termination of
this rebellion, and will hope for success.[17]

Chapter 5

Law and Politics

Just as Lincoln's loyalties were divided between two documents, the US Constitution and the Declaration of Independence, his labor was similarly divided between two professions, law and politics. Law provided his means of financial support, but his greatest interest was always politics. The following speeches and writings illustrate both somber and light-hearted thoughts about these two subjects. The majority of them are from the late 1840s and 1850s.

In this excerpt from a letter to the voters of Sangamon County, published during his first campaign for the legislature in 1832, Lincoln displayed a modest approach to political campaigning.

Fellow-Citizens: Having become a candidate for the honorable office of one of your representatives in the next General Assembly of this State, in accordance with an established custom and the principles of true Republicanism, it becomes my duty to make known to you, the people whom I propose to represent, my sentiments with regard to local affairs.

Time and experience have verified to a demonstration the public utility of internal improvements. That the poorest and most thinly populated countries would be greatly benefited by the opening of good roads, and in the clearing of navigable streams within their limits, is what no person will deny. Yet it is folly to undertake works of this or any other kind without first knowing that we are able to finish them, as half-finished work generally proves to be labor lost. There cannot justly be any objection to having railroads and canals, any more than to other good things, provided they cost nothing. The only objection is to paying for them; and the objection arises from the want of ability to pay. . . .

Upon the subject of education, not presuming to dictate any plan or system respecting it, I can only say that I view it as the most important subject which we as a people can be engaged in. That every man may receive at least a moderate education, and thereby be enabled to read the histories of his own and other countries, by which he may duly appreciate the value of our free institutions, appears to be an object of vital importance, even on this account alone, to say nothing of the advantages and satisfaction to be derived from all being able to read the Scriptures and other works, both of a religious and moral nature, for themselves. For my part, I desire to see the time when education, and by its means, morality, sobriety, enterprise and industry, shall become much more general than at present, and should be gratified to have it in my power to contribute something to the advancement of any measure which might have a tendency to accelerate the happy period. . . .

But, fellow-citizens, I shall conclude. Considering the great degree of modesty which should always attend youth, it is probable I have already been more presuming than becomes me. However, upon the subjects of which I have treated, I have spoken as I have thought. I may be wrong in regard to any or all of them; but, holding it a sound maxim that it is better only sometimes to be right than at all times to be wrong, so soon as I discover my opinions to be erroneous, I shall be ready to renounce them.

Every man is said to have his peculiar ambition. Whether it be true or not, I can say, for one, that I have no other so great as that of being truly esteemed of my fellow-men, by rendering myself worthy of their esteem. How far I shall succeed in gratifying this ambition is yet to be developed. I am young, and unknown to many of you. I was born, and have ever remained, in the most humble walks of life. I have no wealthy or popular relations or friends to recommend me. My case is thrown exclusively upon the independent voters of the county; and, if elected, they will have conferred a favor upon me for which I shall be unremitting in my labors to compensate. But, if the good people in their wisdom shall see fit to keep me in the background, I have been too familiar with disappointments to be very much chagrined.[1]

In his third campaign for the state legislature, Lincoln demonstrated a much more cavalier approach in the announcement of his candidacy than he did in his first campaign.

To the Editor of the "Journal:" In your paper of last Saturday I see a communication, over the signature of "Many Voters," in which the candidates who are announced in the "Journal" are called upon to "show their hands." Agreed. Here's mine.

I go for all sharing the privileges of the government who assist in bearing its burdens. Consequently, I go for admitting all whites to the right of suffrage who pay taxes or bear arms (by no means excluding females).

If elected, I shall consider the whole people of Sangamon my constituents, as well those that oppose as those that support me.

While acting as their representative, I shall be governed by their will on all subjects upon which I have the means of knowing what their will is; and upon all others I shall do what my own judgment teaches me will best advance their interests. Whether elected or not, I go for distributing the proceeds of the sales of the public lands to the several States, to enable our State, in common with others, to dig canals and construct railroads without borrowing money and paying the interest on it.

If alive on the first Monday in November, I shall vote for Hugh L. White for President.[2]

In Lincoln's 1836 campaign for the legislature, a local democrat by the name of Robert Allen started a whispering campaign against him. Allen hinted Lincoln was involved in corrupt activities, but refused to make them public out of pretended deference to Lincoln. Lincoln knew that Allen's implications were groundless, and sent this letter to the Democrat, challenging him to make his accusations public. It proved an effective tactic, as Allen immediately dropped the subject.

Dear Colonel: I am told that during my absence last week you passed through this place, and stated publicly that you were in possession of a fact or facts which, if known to the public, would entirely destroy the prospects of N. W. Edwards and myself at the ensuing election; but that, through favor to us, you should forbear to divulge them. No one has needed favors more than I, and, generally, few have been less unwilling to accept them; but in this case favor to me would be injustice to the public, and therefore I must beg your pardon for declining it. That I once had the confidence of the people of Sangamon, is sufficiently evident; and if I have since done anything, either by design or misadventure, which if known would subject me to a forfeiture of that confidence, he that knows of that thing, and conceals it, is a traitor to his country's interest.

I find myself wholly unable to form any conjecture of what fact or facts, real or supposed, you spoke; but my opinion of your veracity will not permit me for a moment to doubt that you at least believed what you said. I am flattered with the personal regard you manifested for me; but I do hope that on more mature reflection, you will view the public interest as a paramount consideration, and therefore determine to let the worst come. I here assure you that the candid statement of facts on your part, however low it may sink me, shall never break the tie of personal friendship between us. I wish an answer to this, and you are at liberty to publish both, if you choose.[3]

During a debate in the Illinois State Legislature over a banking issue Lincoln made his famous quip about politicians.

Mr. Chairman, this work is exclusively the work of politicians; a set of men who have interests aside from the interests of the people, and who, to say the most of them, are, taken as a mass, at least one long step removed from honest men. I say this with the greater freedom because, being a politician myself, none can regard it as personal.[4]

This photograph of Lincoln was taken on February 27, 1860, the day he delivered his famous Cooper Union Address in New York City.

Library of Congress

Lincoln had become one of the Whig party's political icons in Illinois by the late 1840s, and at the age of 37 was offering political advice.

Now, as to the young men. You must not wait to be brought forward by the older men. For instance, do you suppose that I should have ever got into notice if I had waited to be hunted up and pushed forward by older men? You young men get together and form a "Rough and Ready Club" and have regular meetings and speeches. . . . Let everyone play the part he can play best, some speak, some sing, and all "holler."[5]

In these notes for a law lecture, written sometime in the late 1840s, Lincoln detailed his ethical and functional guidelines for lawyers. He mentioned that fees should be reasonable. Lincoln was infamous among the Sangamon Bar for charging low fees, or giving back money when he thought clients had paid too much. It concludes with his famous statement about the importance of honesty.

I am not an accomplished lawyer. I find quite as much material for a lecture in those points wherein I have failed, as in those wherein I have been moderately successful. The leading rule for the lawyer, as for the man of every other calling, is diligence. Leave nothing for to-morrow which can be done to-day. Never let your correspondence fall behind. Whatever piece of business you have in hand, before stopping, do all the labor pertaining to it which can then be done. When you bring a common-law suit, if you have the facts for doing so, write the declaration at once. If a law point be involved, examine the books, and note the authority you rely on upon the declaration itself, where you are sure to find it when wanted. The same of defenses and pleas. In business not likely to be litigated, ordinary collection cases, foreclosures, partitions, and the like, make all examinations of titles, and note them, and even draft orders and decrees in advance. This course has a triple advantage; it avoids omissions and neglect, saves your labor when once done, performs the labor out of court when you have leisure, rather than in court when you have not. Extemporaneous speaking should be practiced and cultivated. It is the lawyer's avenue to the public. However able and faithful he may be in other respects, people are slow to bring him business if he cannot make a speech. And yet there is not a more fatal error to young lawyers than relying too much on speech-making. If any one, upon his rare powers of speaking, shall claim an exemption from the drudgery of the law, his case is a failure in advance.

Discourage litigation. Persuade your neighbors to compromise whenever you can. Point out to them how the nominal winner is often a real loser—in fees, expenses, and waste of time. As a peacemaker the lawyer has a superior opportunity of being a good man. There will still be business enough.

Never stir up litigation. A worse man can scarcely be found than one who does this. Who can be more nearly a fiend than he who habitually overhauls the register of deeds in search of defects in titles, whereon to stir up strife, and put money in his pocket? A moral tone ought to be infused into the profession which should drive such men out of it.

The matter of fees is important, far beyond the mere question of bread and butter involved. Properly attended to, fuller justice is done to both lawyer and client. An exorbitant fee should never be claimed. As a general rule never take your whole fee in advance, nor any more than a small retainer. When fully paid beforehand, you are more than a common mortal if you can feel the same interest in the case, as if something was still in prospect for you, as well as for your client. And when you lack interest in the case the job will very likely lack skill and diligence in the performance. Settle the amount of fee and take a note in advance. Then you will feel that you are working for something, and you are sure to do your work faithfully and well. Never sell a fee note—at least not before the consideration service is performed. It leads to negligence and dishonesty—negligence by losing interest in the case, and dishonesty in refusing to refund when you have allowed the consideration to fail.

There is a vague popular belief that lawyers are necessarily dishonest. I say vague, because when we consider to what extent confidence and honors are reposed in and conferred upon lawyers by the people, it appears improbable that their impression of dishonesty is very distinct and vivid. Yet the impression is common, almost universal. Let no young man choosing the law for a calling for a moment yield to the popular belief— resolve to be honest at all events; and if in your own judgment you cannot be an honest lawyer, resolve to be honest without being a lawyer. Choose some other occupation, rather than one in the choosing of which you do, in advance, consent to be a knave.[6]

While in Congress Lincoln made one of the longer political speeches of his career, which was basically a lampooning of the Democratic Party and its leaders. In addition to the political sarcasm, he earnestly preached the superiority of the Whig position.

You Democrats, and your candidate, in the main are in favor of laying down in advance a platform—a set of party positions—as a unit, and then of forcing the people, by every sort of appliance, to ratify them, however unpalatable some of them may be. We and our candidate are in favor of making presidential elections, and the legislation of the country distinct matters; so that the people can elect whom they please, and afterward legislate just as they please, without any hindrance, save only so much as may guard against infractions of the Constitution, undue haste, and want of consideration. The difference between us is clear as noonday. That we are right we cannot doubt. We hold the true Republican position. In leaving the people's business in their hands, we cannot be wrong. We are willing, and even anxious, to go to the people on this issue.

. . .You [democrats] violated the primary, the cardinal, the one great living principle of all democratic representative government—the principle that the representative is bound to carry out the known will of his constituents. . . .

By the way, Mr. Speaker, did you know I am a military hero? Yes, sir; in the days of the Black Hawk war I fought, bled, and came away. Speaking of General Cass's career reminds me of my own. I was not at Stillman's defeat, but I was about as near it as Cass was to Hull's surrender; and, like him, I saw the place very soon afterward. It is quite certain I did not break my sword, for I had none to break; but I bent a musket pretty badly on one occasion. If Cass broke his sword, the idea is he broke it in desperation; I bent the musket by accident. If General Cass went in advance of me in picking huckleberries, I guess I surpassed him in charges upon the wild onions. If he saw any live, fighting Indians, it was more than I did; but I had a good many bloody struggles with the mosquitoes, and although I never fainted from the loss of blood, I can truly say I was often very hungry. Mr. Speaker, if I should ever conclude to doff whatever our Democratic friends may suppose there is of black-cockade federalism about me, and therefore they shall take me up as their candidate for the presidency, I protest they shall not make fun of me, as they have of General Cass, by attempting to write me into a military hero.[7]

A couple of months later, Lincoln made another speech in Congress, this time ridiculing the Democratic Party of New York.

I have heard some things from New York; and if they are true, one might well say of your party there, as a drunken fellow once said when he heard the reading of an indictment for hogstealing. The clerk read on till he got to and through the words, "did steal, take, and carry away ten boars, ten sows, ten shoats, and ten pigs," at which he exclaimed, "Well, by golly, that is the most equally divided gang of hogs I ever did hear of!" If there is any other gang of hogs more equally divided than the Democrats of New York are about this time, I have not heard of it.[8]

In his eulogy of Henry Clay, Lincoln criticized politicians that attempted to run for office as independents.

A free people in times of peace and quiet—when pressed by no common danger—naturally divide into parties. At such times the man who is of neither party is not, cannot be, of any consequence.[9]

Stephen A. Douglas, Lincoln's long-time political rival, taken during the Lincoln-Douglas debates.

National Archives

One of Lincoln's favorite tactics in political debate was to carefully research the speeches of his opponents and use their own words to embarrass them on the subject in question. An example of this is in Lincoln's ridicule of what Stephen Douglas said about the Declaration's statement "all men are created equal."

Now let us hear Judge Douglas's view of the same subject, as I find it in the printed report of his late speech. Here it is:

"No man can vindicate the character, motives, and conduct of the signers of the Declaration of Independence, except upon the hypothesis that they referred to the white race alone, and not to the African, when they declared all men to have been created equal; that they were speaking of British subjects on this continent being equal to British subjects born and residing in Great Britain; that they were entitled to the same inalienable rights, and among them were enumerated life, liberty, and the pursuit of happiness. The Declaration was adopted for the purpose of justifying the colonists in the eyes of the civilized world in withdrawing their allegiance from the British crown, and dissolving their connection with the mother country."

My good friends, read that carefully over some leisure hour, and ponder well upon it; see what a mere wreck—mangled ruin — it makes of our once glorious Declaration.

"They were speaking of British subjects on this continent being equal to British subjects born and residing in Great Britain!" Why, according to this, not only Negroes but white people outside of Great Britain and America were not spoken of in that instrument. The English, Irish, and Scotch, along with white Americans, were included, to be sure, but the French, Germans, and other white people of the world are all gone to pot along with the judge's inferior races!

I had thought the Declaration promised something better than the condition of British subjects; but no, it only meant that we should be equal to them in their own oppressed and unequal condition. According to that, it gave no promise that, having kicked off the king and lords of Great Britain, we should not at once be saddled with a king and lords of our own.

I had thought the Declaration contemplated the progressive improvement in the condition of all men everywhere; but no, it merely "was adopted for the purpose of justifying the colonists in the eyes of the civilized world in withdrawing their allegiance from the British crown, and dissolving their connection with the mother country." Why, that object having been effected some eighty years ago, the Declaration is of no practical use now—mere rubbish—old wadding left to rot on the battle-field after the victory is won.

I understand you are preparing to celebrate the "Fourth," to-morrow week. What for? The doings of that day had no reference to the present; and quite half of you are not even descendants of those who were referred to at that day. But I suppose you will celebrate, and will even go so far as to read the Declaration. Suppose, after you read it once in the old-fashioned way, you read it once more with Judge Douglas's version. It will then run thus: "We hold these truths to be self-evident, that all British subjects who were on this continent eighty-one years ago, were created equal to all British subjects born and then residing in Great Britain."

And now I appeal to all—to Democrats as well as others—are you really willing that the Declaration shall thus be frittered away?—thus left no more, at most, than an interesting memorial of the dead past?—thus shorn of its vitality and practical value, and left without the germ or even the suggestion of the individual rights of man in it?[10]

In 1858 Lincoln criticized noisy presidential nominating conventions. Two years later, the Republican Convention in Chicago that nominated him would be one of the noisiest to date.

I think too much reliance is placed in noisy demonstrations, importing speakers from a distance and the like. They excite prejudice and close the avenues to sober reason. The "home production" principle in my judgment is the best.[11]

By the late 1850s, Lincoln was a superior stump speaker. In the following he combined humor, self-deprecation, and mock deference to the superiority of his political opponent in order to simultaneously entertain the audience and make his point.

There is still another disadvantage under which we labor, and to which I will ask your attention. It arises out of the relative positions of the two persons who stand before the State as candidates for the Senate. Senator Douglas is of world-wide renown. All the anxious politicians of his party, or who have been of his party for years past, have been looking upon him as certainly, at no distant day, to be the President of the United States. They have seen in his round, jolly, fruitful face, post-offices, land-offices, marshal ships, and cabinet appointments, charge ships and foreign missions, bursting and sprouting out in wonderful exuberance, ready to be laid hold of by their greedy hands. And as they have been gazing upon this attractive picture so long, they cannot, in the little distraction that has taken place in the party, bring themselves to give up the charming hope; but with greedier anxiety they rush about him, sustain him, and give him marches, triumphal entries, and receptions beyond what even in the days of his highest prosperity they could have brought about in his favor. On the contrary, nobody has ever expected me to be President. In my poor, lean, lank face nobody has ever seen that any cabbages were sprouting out. These are disadvantages all, taken together, that the Republicans labor under. We have to fight this battle upon principle, and upon principle alone. I am, in a certain sense, made the standard-bearer in behalf of the Republicans. . . .[12]

The following includes Lincoln's famous satire about "homeopathic soup," describing how thin Judge Douglas' political arguments about Popular Sovereignty had become.

The truth about the matter is this: Judge Douglas has sung paeans to his "popular sovereignty" doctrine until his Supreme Court, cooperating with him, has squatted his squatter sovereignty out. But he will keep up this species of humbuggery about squatter sovereignty. He has at last invented this sort of do-nothing sovereignty—that the people may exclude slavery by a sort of "sovereignty" that is exercised by doing nothing at all. Is not that running his popular sovereignty down awfully? Has it not got down as thin as the homeopathic soup that was made by boiling the shadow of a Pigeon that had starved to death? But at last, when it is brought to the test of close reasoning, there is not even that thin decoction of it left. It is a presumption impossible in the domain of thought. It is precisely no other than the putting of that most unphilosophical proposition, that two bodies can occupy the same space at the same time.

The Dred Scott decision covers the whole ground, and while it occupies it, there is no room even for the shadow of a starved pigeon to occupy the same ground.[13]

Lincoln combined the memory of Thomas Jefferson with humor to berate the Democratic Party. This is an example of why Douglas once said: "Every one of his stories seems like a whack across my back. . . . Nothing else—not any of his arguments or any of his replies to my questions—disturbs me. But when he begins to tell a story, I feel that I am to be overmatched."[14]

Remembering, too, that the Jefferson party was formed upon its supposed superior devotion to the personal rights of men, holding the rights of property to be secondary only, and greatly inferior, and assuming that the so-called Democracy of to-day are the Jefferson, and their opponents the anti-Jefferson party, it will be equally interesting to note how completely the two have changed hands as to the principle upon which they were originally supposed to be divided.

The Democracy of to-day hold the liberty of one man to be absolutely nothing, when in conflict with another man's right of property; Republicans, on the contrary, are for both the man and the dollar, but in case of conflict the man before the dollar.

I remember being once much amused at seeing two partially intoxicated men engaged in a fight with their great-coats on, which fight, after a long and rather harmless contest, ended in each having fought himself out of his own coat and into that of the other. If the two leading parties of this day are really identical with the two in the days of Jefferson and Adams, they have performed the same feat as the two drunken men.[15]

In 1860, Lincoln was still providing law advice. In the following letter he responded to a young man that had asked him how to become a lawyer.

Dear Sir: Yours of the 24th. asking "the best mode of obtaining a thorough knowledge of the law" is received. The mode is very simple, though laborious, and tedious. It is only to get the books, and read, and study them carefully. Begin with Blackstone's Commentaries, and after reading it carefully through, say twice, take up Chitty's Pleading, Greenleaf's Evidence, & Story's Equity &c. in succession. Work, work, work, is the main thing.[16]

Lincoln demonstrated he held no grudges against those that opposed him at the ballot box.

In all our rejoicings, let us neither express nor cherish any hard feelings toward any citizen who, by his vote, has differed with us. Let us at all times remember that all American citizens are brothers of a common country, and should do well together in the bonds of fraternal feeling.[17]

Lincoln voiced a political maxim that was well known, even in his day.

It is not the qualified voters, but the qualified voters who choose to vote, that constitute the political power of a state.[18]

Chapter 6

Freedom

Lincoln was considered a "moderate" on the slavery issue. He believed slavery was a moral evil, and spoke out against it for most of his adult life. Rather than insisting it be immediately ended as abolitionists did, he was willing to allow it to die slowly, and to aid in this insisted that it be prevented from spreading into the territories. Lincoln personally hoped that one day the black man would have true equality with the white, but he believed that because of the prejudice of the white race, this would not be realized for a long time. Most of Lincoln's most memorable speeches, some of which are presented here, are centered around the struggle to end slavery and give the black man the right "to eat the bread he earned."

As a young legislator in 1837, Lincoln and another state representative drafted a document protesting recent legislative resolutions supporting slavery. Although they softened their protest by complaining about the rhetoric of abolitionists and acknowledging the Constitution's protection of slavery, it was still a bold step for politicians of that era.

Resolutions upon the subject of domestic slavery having passed both branches of the General Assembly at its present session, the undersigned hereby protest against the passage of the same.

They believe that the institution of slavery is founded on both injustice and bad policy, but that the promulgation of Abolition doctrines tends rather to increase than abate its evils. They believe that the Congress of the United States has no power under the Constitution to interfere with the institution of slavery in the different States. They believe that the Congress of the United States has the power, under the Constitution, to abolish slavery in the District of Columbia, but that the power ought not to be exercised unless at the request of the people of the District. The difference between these opinions and those contained in the above resolutions is their reason for entering this protest.[1]

Lincoln's arguments about freedom were not limited to America and the black race. In September 1849 Lincoln became intrigued with events in Hungary, where freedom fighters had been suppressed by their government during the Hungarian Revolution of 1848. Lincoln and a group of citizens of Springfield passed the following resolutions in behalf of the freedom fighters, expressing both moral support and understanding of America's limited influence in Europe.

Resolved:

1. That it is the right of any people, sufficiently numerous for national independence, to throw off, to revolutionize, their existing form of government, and to establish such other in its stead as they may choose.

2. That it is the duty of our government to neither foment, nor assist, such revolutions in other governments.

3. That, as we may not legally or warrantably interfere abroad, to aid, so no other government may interfere abroad, to suppress such revolutions; and that we should at once, announce to the world, our determination to insist upon this mutuality of non-intervention, as a sacred principle of the international law. . . .[2]

In the 1850s, Southern writers, editors, and preachers proclaimed the advantages the slaves of America had over the black people of Africa. Lincoln pointed out the folly of this with the following observation.

Although volume upon volume is written to prove slavery a very good thing, we never hear of a man who wishes to take the good of it by being a slave himself.[3]

The following is from what many consider to be Lincoln's first great speech on the subject of freedom. Made in Peoria, Illinois, in October of 1854, Lincoln replied to Douglas' statement that the latter was essentially indifferent to what the people of the territories thought of slavery. In this speech Lincoln presented one of the fundamental arguments against slavery that he would repeat many times over the years. This was, that if the black man was in fact a man, rather than something less, he believed "all men are created equal" and he should be treated like everyone else.

This declared indifference . . . for the spread of slavery, I cannot but hate. I hate it because of the monstrous injustice of slavery itself. I hate it because it deprives our republican example of its just influence in the world; enables the enemies of free institutions with plausibility to taunt us as hypocrites; causes the real friends of freedom to doubt our sincerity; and especially because it forces so many good men among ourselves into an open war with the very fundamental principles of civil liberty, criticizing the Declaration of Independence, and insisting that there is no right principle of action but self-interest. . . .

The doctrine of self-government is right—absolutely and eternally right, but it has no just application as here attempted. Or perhaps I should rather say that whether it has such application depends upon whether a Negro is not or is a man. If he is not a man, in that case he who is a man may as a matter of self-government do just what he pleases with him. But if the Negro is a man, is it not to that extent a total destruction of self-government to say that he too shall not govern himself? When the white man governs himself, that is self-government; but when he governs himself and also governs another man, that is more than self-government—that is despotism. If the Negro is a man, why then my ancient faith teaches me that "all men are created equal," and that there can be no moral right in connection with one man's making a slave of another. . . .

. . . What I do say is that no man is good enough to govern another man without that other's consent. I say this is the leading principle, the sheet-anchor of American republicanism. Our Declaration of Independence says:

"We hold these truths to be self-evident: That all men are created equal; that they are endowed by their Creator with certain inalienable rights; that among these are life, liberty, and the pursuit of happiness. That to secure these rights, governments are instituted among men, deriving their just powers from the consent of the governed."

I have quoted so much at this time merely to show that, according to our ancient faith, the just powers of governments are derived from the consent of the governed. Now the relation of master and slave is pro tanto a total violation of this principle. The master not only governs the slave without his consent, but he governs him by a set of rules altogether different from those which he prescribes for himself. Allow all the governed an equal voice in the government, and that, and that only, is self-government. . . .

. . . Fellow-countrymen, Americans, South as well as North, shall we make no effort to arrest this? Already the liberal party throughout the world express the apprehension "that the one retrograde institution in America is undermining the principles of progress, and fatally violating the noblest political system the world ever saw." This is not the taunt of enemies, but the warning of friends. Is it quite safe to disregard it—to despise it? Is there no danger to liberty itself in discarding the earliest practice and first precept of our ancient faith? In our greedy chase to make profit of the Negro, let us beware lest we "cancel and tear in pieces" even the white man's charter of freedom.

Our republican robe is soiled and trailed in the dust. Let us repurify it. Let us turn and wash it white in the spirit, if not the blood, of the Revolution. Let us turn slavery from its claims of "moral right" back upon its existing legal rights and its arguments of "necessity." Let us return it to the position our fathers gave it, and there let it rest in peace. Let us readopt the Declaration of Independence, and with it the practices and policy which harmonize with it. Let North and South—let all Americans—let all lovers of liberty everywhere join in the great and good work. If we do this, we shall not only have saved the Union, but we shall have so saved it as to make and to keep it forever worthy of the saving. We shall have so saved it that the succeeding millions of free happy people, the world over, shall rise up and call us blessed to the latest generations.[4]

In this letter to an elderly Kentuckian that had been congressman during the passage of the Missouri Compromise, Lincoln expressed his belief that the United States was moving away from, rather than approaching, the nation's founders' plan of gradual abolishment of slavery.

There is no peaceful extinction of slavery in prospect for us. The signal failure of Henry Clay and other good and great men, in 1849, to effect anything in favor of gradual emancipation in Kentucky, together with a thousand other signs, extinguished that hope utterly. On the question of liberty as a principle, we are not what we have been. When we were the political slaves of King George, and wanted to be free, we called the maxim that "all men are created equal" a self-evident truth, but now when we have grown fat, and have lost all dread of being slaves ourselves, we have become so greedy to be masters that we call the same maxim "a self-evident lie." The Fourth of July has not quite dwindled away; it is still a great day—for burning fire-crackers!!!

That spirit which desired the peaceful extinction of slavery has itself become extinct with the occasion and the men of the Revolution. Under the impulse of that occasion, nearly half the States adopted systems of emancipation at once, and it is a significant fact that not a single State has done the like since. So far as peaceful voluntary emancipation is concerned, the condition of the Negro slave in America, scarcely less terrible to the contemplation of a free mind, is now as fixed and hopeless of change for the better, as that of the lost souls of the finally impenitent. The Autocrat of all the Russias will resign his crown and proclaim his subjects free republicans sooner than will our American masters voluntarily give up their slaves.

Our political problem now is, "Can we as a nation continue together permanently—forever half slave and half free?" The problem is too mighty for me—may God, in his mercy, superintend the solution.[5]

In August of 1855 Lincoln wrote a letter to his friend Joshua Speed, who had moved from Springfield to Kentucky several years previously. In this correspondence, Lincoln described to the proslavery Speed his hatred of slavery, his reason for controlling his feelings about it, and his disappointment with the American people's failure to condemn it.

You know how I dislike slavery, and you fully admit the abstract wrong of it. . . . But you say that sooner than yield your legal right to the slave, especially at the bidding of those who are not themselves interested, you would see the Union dissolved. I am not aware that any one is bidding you yield that right; very certainly I am not. I leave that matter entirely to yourself. I also acknowledge your rights and my obligations under the Constitution in regard to your slaves. I confess I hate to see the poor creatures hunted down and caught and carried back to their stripes and unrequited toil; but I bite my lips and keep quiet.

In 1841 you and I had together a tedious low water trip on a steamboat from Louisville to St. Louis. You may remember, as I well do, that from Louisville to the mouth of the Ohio there were on board ten or a dozen slaves shackled together with irons. That sight was a continued torment to me, and I see something like it every time I touch the Ohio or any other slaver border. It is not fair for you to assume that I have no interest in a thing which has, and continually exercises, the power of making me miserable. You ought rather to appreciate how much the great body of the Northern people do crucify their feelings, in order to maintain their loyalty to the Constitution and the Union. I do oppose the extension of slavery because my judgment and feeling so prompt me, and I am under no obligations to the contrary. If for this you and I must differ, differ we must. . . .

You inquire where I now stand. That is a disputed point. I think I am a Whig; but others say there are no Whigs, and that I am an Abolitionist. When I was at Washington, I voted for the Wilmot proviso as good as forty times; and I never heard of any one attempting to unwhig me for that. I now do no more than oppose the extension of slavery. I am not a Know-Nothing;[6] that is certain. How could I be? How can any one who abhors the oppression of Negroes be in favor of degrading classes of white people? Our progress in degeneracy appears to me to be pretty rapid. As a nation we began by declaring that "all men are created equal." We now practically read it "all men are created equal, except Negroes." When the Know-Nothings get control, it will read "all men are created equal, except Negroes and foreigners and Catholics." When it comes to this, I shall prefer emigrating to some country where they make no pretense of loving liberty—to Russia, for instance, where despotism can be taken pure, and without the base alloy of hypocrisy.[7]

In discussing colonization of blacks to Liberia, Lincoln presented his belief that the black man is a man, and his bondage wrong.

How differently the respective courses of the Democratic and Republican parties incidentally bear on the question of forming a will—a public sentiment—for colonization, is easy to see. The Republicans inculcate, with whatever of ability they can, that the Negro is a man, that his bondage is cruelly wrong, and that the field of his oppression ought not to be enlarged. The Democrats deny his manhood; deny, or dwarf to insignificance, the wrong of his bondage; so far as possible, crush all sympathy for him, and cultivate and excite hatred and disgust against him; compliment themselves as Union-savers for doing so; and call the indefinite outspreading of his bondage "a sacred right of self-government."[8]

In a June 1857 speech in Springfield, Lincoln responded to Douglas' declaration that freedom to the black man would mean "amalgamation" of the races. The amalgamation arguments between Lincoln and Douglas illustrated more effectively than any other the prevalent racist attitudes of whites in the mid-19th century. On the one side was Stephen A. Douglas—a leading Democrat—declaring that the black man was sub-human and unworthy of ever approaching social equality with the white man. Arguing against him was Lincoln, agreeing that the black man was not currently the white man's social equal but stating that he nevertheless was human, and had the right to "eat the bread he earns."

There is a natural disgust in the minds of nearly all white people at the idea of an indiscriminate amalgamation of the white and black races; and Judge Douglas evidently is basing his chief hope upon the chances of his being able to appropriate the benefit of this disgust to himself. If he can, by much drumming and repeating, fasten the odium of that idea upon his adversaries, he thinks he can struggle through the storm. He therefore clings to this hope, as a drowning man to the last plank. He makes an occasion for lugging it in from the opposition to the Dred Scott decision. He finds the Republicans insisting that the Declaration of Independence includes all men, black as well as white, and forthwith he boldly denies that it includes Negroes at all, and proceeds to argue gravely that all who contend it does, do so only because they want to vote, and eat, and sleep, and marry with Negroes! He will have it that they cannot be consistent else. Now I protest against the counterfeit logic which concludes that, because I do not want a black woman for a slave I must necessarily want her for a wife. I need not have her for either. I can just leave her alone. In some respects she certainly is not my equal; but in her natural right to eat the bread she earns with her own hands without asking leave of any one else, she is my equal, and the equal of all others.[9]

On June 16, 1858, at the Republican State Convention in Springfield, Lincoln was declared his party's choice to run against Stephen A. Douglas in the upcoming Senate campaign. It was at this convention that Lincoln made his famous "House Divided" speech, in which he used a biblical analogy declaring the nation would not be able to continue "half slave and half free."

Mr. President and Gentlemen of the Convention: If we could first know where we are, and whither we are tending, we could better judge what to do, and how to do it. We are now far into the fifth year since a policy was initiated with the avowed object and confident promise of putting an end to slavery agitation. Under the operation of that policy, that agitation has not only not ceased, but has constantly augmented. In my opinion, it will not cease until a crisis shall have been reached and passed.

"A house divided against itself cannot stand." I believe this government cannot endure permanently half slave and half free. I do not expect the Union to be dissolved—I do not expect the house to fall—but I do expect it will cease to be divided. It will become all one thing, or all the other. Either the opponents of slavery will arrest the further spread of it, and place it where the public mind shall rest in the belief that it is in the course of ultimate extinction; or its advocates will push it forward till it shall become alike lawful in all the States, old as well as new, North as well as South."[10]

In Chicago, shortly before the Lincoln-Douglas debates, Lincoln revealed the primary arguments he would use against slavery, Douglas, and the Democratic Party in the coming months.

Now, sirs, for the purpose of squaring things with this [Douglas'] idea of "don't care if slavery is voted up or voted down," for sustaining the Dred Scott decision, for holding that the Declaration of Independence did not mean anything at all, we have Judge Douglas giving his exposition of what the Declaration of Independence means, and we have him saying that the people of America are equal to the people of Britain. According to his construction, you Germans are not connected with it. Now I ask you, in all soberness, if all these things, if indulged in, if ratified, if confirmed and indorsed, if taught to our children, and repeated to them, do not tend to rub out the sentiment of liberty in the country, and to transform this government into a government of some other form? Those arguments that are made, that the inferior race are to be treated with as much allowance as they are capable of enjoying; that as much is to be done for them as their condition will allow—what are these arguments? They are the arguments that kings have made for enslaving the people in all ages of the world. You will find that all the arguments in favor of kingcraft were of this class; they always bestrode the necks of the people—not that they wanted to do it, but because the people were better off for being ridden. That is their argument, and this argument of the judge is the same old serpent that says, You work and I eat, you toil and I will enjoy the fruits of it.

Turn in whatever way you will—whether it come from the mouth of a king, an excuse for enslaving the people of his country, or from the mouth of men of one race as a reason for enslaving the men of another race, it is all the same old serpent, and I hold if that course of argumentation that is made for the purpose of convincing the public mind that we should not care about this should be granted, it does not stop with the Negro. I should like to know—taking this old Declaration of Independence, which declares that all men are equal upon principle, and making exceptions to it—where will it stop? If one man says it does not mean a Negro, why not another say it does not mean some other man?

If that Declaration is not the truth, let us get the statute-book in which we find it, and tear it out! Who is so bold as to do it? If it is not true, let us tear it out. Let us stick to it, then; let us stand firmly by it, then.

It may be argued that there are certain conditions that make necessities and impose them upon us, and to the extent that a necessity is imposed upon a man, he must submit to it. I think that was the condition in which we found ourselves when we established this government. We had slaves among us; we could not get our Constitution unless we permitted them to remain in slavery; we could not secure the good we did secure if we grasped for more; but having by necessity submitted to that much, it does not destroy the principle that is the charter of our liberties. Let that charter stand as our standard. . . .

My friends, I have detained you about as long as I desired to do, and I have only to say, let us discard all this quibbling about this man and the other man—this race and that race and the other race being inferior, and therefore they must be placed in an inferior position—discarding our standard that we have left us. Let us discard all these things, and unite as one people throughout this land, until we shall once more stand up declaring that all men are created equal.[11]

In Springfield, Lincoln explained his perception of why the formers of the government allowed slavery to continue and how they planned for its eventual end. He also discussed a plan that he would later pursue experimentally as president— separation of the races. This is the last speech he made before challenging Douglas to debate.

Although I have ever been opposed to slavery, so far I rested in the hope and belief that it was in the course of ultimate extinction. For that reason, it had been a minor question with me. I might have been mistaken; but I had believed, and now believe, that the whole public mind, that is, the mind of the great majority, had rested in that belief up to the repeal of the Missouri Compromise. But upon that event, I became convinced that either I had been resting in a delusion, or the institution was being placed on a new basis—a basis for making it perpetual, national, and universal. Subsequent events have greatly confirmed me in that belief. I believe that bill to be the beginning of a conspiracy for that purpose. So believing, I have since then considered that question a paramount one. So believing, I think the public mind will never rest till the power of Congress to restrict the spread of it shall again be acknowledged and exercised on the one hand, or, on the other, all resistance be entirely crushed out. I have expressed that opinion, and I entertain it to-night. It is denied that there is any tendency to the nationalization of slavery in these States.

. . . My declarations upon this subject of Negro slavery may be misrepresented, but cannot be misunderstood. I have said that I do not understand the Declaration to mean that all men were created equal in all respects. They are not our equal in color; but I suppose that it does mean to declare that all men are equal in some respects; they are equal in their right to "life, liberty, and the pursuit of happiness." Certainly the Negro is not our equal in color—perhaps not in many other respects; still, in the right to put into his mouth the bread that his own hands have earned, he is the equal of every other man, white or black. In pointing out that more has been given you, you cannot be justified in taking away the little which has been given him. All I ask for the Negro is that if you do not like him, let him alone. If God gave him but little, that little let him enjoy.

When our government was established, we had the institution of slavery among us. We were in a certain sense compelled to tolerate its existence. It was a sort of necessity. We had gone through our struggle, and secured our own independence. The framers of the Constitution found the institution of slavery amongst their other institutions at the time. They found that by an effort to eradicate it, they might lose much of what they had already gained. They were obliged to bow to the necessity. They gave power to Congress to abolish the slave-trade at the end of twenty years. They also prohibited slavery in the Territories where it did not exist. They did what they could and yielded to necessity for the rest. I also yield to all which follows from that necessity. What I would most desire would be the separation of the white and black races.[12]

At Ottawa, first of the seven Lincoln-Douglas debates, Douglas pressed an attack upon Lincoln, exaggerating the latter's statements and trying to convince the audience that Lincoln was in favor of immediate social equality of the races. Lincoln responded with the popular concept of the day—that absolute equality may never be achieved because of differences in the races. He also spoke against the currently unrealistic idea of immediately abolishing slavery in the Southern states. He then went on to say that he was still in favor of granting the black race the rights expressed in the Declaration of Independence.

Now, gentlemen, I don't want to read at any great length, but this is the true complexion of all I have ever said in regard to the institution of slavery and the black race. This is the whole of it, and anything that argues me into his idea of perfect social and political equality with the Negro is but a specious and fantastic arrangement of words, by which a man can prove a horse-chestnut to be a chestnut horse. I will say here, while upon this subject, that I have no purpose, either directly or indirectly, to interfere with the institution of slavery in the States where it exists. I believe I have no lawful right to do so, and I have no inclination to do so. I have no purpose to introduce political and social equality between the white and the black races. There is a physical difference between the two, which, in my judgment, will probably forever forbid their living together upon the footing of perfect equality; and inasmuch as it becomes a necessity that there must be a difference, I, as well as Judge Douglas, am in favor of the race to which I belong having the superior position. I have never said anything to the contrary, but I hold that, notwithstanding all this, there is no reason in the world why the Negro is not entitled to all the natural rights enumerated in the Declaration of Independence—the right to life, liberty, and the pursuit of happiness. I hold that he is as much entitled to these as the white man. I agree with Judge Douglas he is not my equal in many respects— certainly not in color, perhaps not in moral or intellectual endowment. But in the right to eat the bread, without the leave of anybody else, which his own hand earns, he is my equal and the equal of Judge Douglas, and the equal of every living man.[13]

In the debate at Charleston, Lincoln revealed his belief as to how long it would take to eliminate slavery. He obviously didn't foresee Civil War:

There is no way of putting an end to the slavery agitation amongst us but to put it back upon the basis where our fathers placed it, no way but to keep it out of our new Territories—to restrict it forever to the old States where it now exists. Then the public mind will rest in the belief that it is in the course of ultimate extinction. That is one way of putting an end to the slavery agitation.

The other way is for us to surrender and let Judge Douglas and his friends have their way and plant slavery over all the States—cease speaking of it as in any way a wrong—regard slavery as one of the common matters of property, and speak of negroes as we do of our horses and cattle. But while it drives on in its state of progress as it is now driving, and as it has driven for the last five years, I have ventured the opinion, and I say today, that we will have no end to the slavery agitation until it takes one turn or the other. I do not mean that when it takes a turn towards ultimate extinction it will be in a day, nor in a year, nor in two years. I do not suppose that in the most peaceful way ultimate extinction would occur in less than a hundred years at the least; but that it will occur in the best way for both races in God's own good time, I have no doubt.[14]

In the debate at Galesburg, Lincoln argued against Douglas' position that African Americans were not included in the Declaration of Independence.

The Judge has alluded to the Declaration of Independence, and insisted that Negroes are not included in that Declaration; and that it is a slander upon the framers of that instrument to suppose that Negroes were meant therein; and he asks you: Is it possible to believe that Mr. Jefferson, who penned the immortal paper, could have supposd himself applying the language of that instrument to the Negro race, and yet held a portion of that race in slavery? Would he not at once have freed them? I only have to remark upon this part of the Judge's speech, . . . that I believe the entire records of the world, from the date of the Declaration of Independence up to within three years ago, may be searched in vain for one single affirmation, from one single man, that the Negro was not included in the Declaration of Independence.[15]

On election day, November 2, 1858, the Democrats successfully retained a majority in the state legislature, thereby assuring Douglas would defeat Lincoln in the senate election the following January.[16] Writing to a political associate, Lincoln showed characteristic perseverance in declaring that the fight against slavery must continue in spite of his defeat.

The fight must go on. The cause of civil liberty must not be surrendered at the end of one or even one hundred defeats.[17]

After losing the senate race to Douglas, Lincoln tells a friend he is glad that he had an opportunity to strike a blow at slavery before he was "forgotten."

I am glad I made the late race. It gave me a hearing on the great and durable question of the age, which I could have had in no other way; and though I now sink out of view, and shall be forgotten, I believe I have made some marks which will tell for the cause of civil liberty long after I am gone.[18]

Lincoln, after his defeat by Douglas, continued to express his concern the country was on a destructive path regarding freedom and propagation of slavery. Here he proclaimed the principles of Jefferson while deriding those that talk about "superior races."

Bearing in mind that about seventy years ago two great political parties were first formed in this country, that Thomas Jefferson was the head of one of them and Boston the headquarters of the other, it is both curious and interesting that those supposed to descend politically from the party opposed to Jefferson should now be celebrating his birthday in their own original seat of empire, while those claiming political descent from him have nearly ceased to breathe his name everywhere. . . .

. . . But, soberly, it is now no child's play to save the principles of Jefferson from total overthrow in this nation. One would state with great confidence that he could convince any sane child that the simpler propositions of Euclid are true; but nevertheless he would fail, utterly, with one who should deny the definitions and axioms. The principles of Jefferson are the definitions and axioms of free society. And yet they are denied and evaded, with no small show of success. One dashingly calls them "glittering generalities." Another bluntly calls them "self-evident lies." And others insidiously argue that they apply to "superior races." These expressions, differing in form, are identical in object and effect—the supplanting the principles of free government, and restoring those of classification, caste, and legitimacy. They would delight a convocation of crowned heads plotting against the people. They are the vanguard, the miners and sappers of returning despotism. We must repulse them, or they will subjugate us.

This is a world of compensation; and he who would be no slave must consent to have no slave. Those who deny freedom to others deserve it not for themselves, and, under a just God, cannot long retain it.

All honor to Jefferson—to the man who, in the concrete pressure of a struggle for national independence by a single people, had the coolness, forecast, and capacity to introduce into a merely revolutionary document an abstract truth, applicable to all men and all times, and so to embalm it there that to-day and in all coming days it shall be a rebuke and a stumbling-block to the very harbingers of reappearing tyranny and oppression.[19]

In these notes for a speech in Ohio in 1859, Lincoln took the position that slavery must be allowed to continue where it currently existed because the Constitution allowed it. However, he restated the people should remain true to the main purpose—the gradual, inevitable destruction of slavery.

We must not disturb slavery in the states where it exists, because the constitution, and the peace of the country, both forbid us. We must not withhold an efficient fugitive slave law, because the constitution demands it.

But we must, by a national policy, prevent the spread of slavery into new territories, or free states, because the constitution does not forbid us, and the general welfare does demand such prevention. We must prevent the revival of the African slave trade, because the constitution does not forbid us, and the general welfare does require the prevention. We must prevent these things being done by either congresses or courts. The people— the people—are the rightful masters of both congresses, and courts—not to overthrow the constitution, but to overthrow the men who pervert it.

To effect our main object, we have to employ auxiliary means. We must hold conventions, adopt platforms, select candidates, and carry elections. At every step we must be true to the main purpose. If we adopt a platform, falling short of our principle, or elect a man rejecting our principle, we not only take nothing affirmative by our success; but we draw upon us the positive embarrassment of seeming ourselves to have abandoned our principle.

That our principle, however baffled, or delayed, will finally triumph, I do not permit myself to doubt. Men will pass away—die—die, politically, and naturally; but the principle will live, and live forever. Organizations, rallied around that principle, may, by their own dereliction, go to pieces, thereby losing all their time and labor. But the principle will remain, and will reproduce another, and another, till the final triumph will come.

But to bring it soon, we must save our labor already performed—our organization, which has cost so much time and toil to create. We must keep our principle constantly in view, and never be false to it.

And as to men, for leaders, we must remember that "He that is not for us, is against us;" and "he that gathereth not with us scattereth."[20]

In the following speech in Cincinnati on September 17, 1859, Lincoln uses humor to communicate both his belief slavery is morally wrong and his doubts that the South could successfully leave the Union.

It has occurred to me here to-night, that if I ever do shoot over the line at the people on the other side of the line into a Slave State, and purpose to do so, keeping my skin safe, that I have now about the best chance I shall ever have. I should not wonder that there are some Kentuckians about this audience; we are close to Kentucky; and whether that be so or not, we are on elevated ground, and by speaking distinctly, I should not wonder if some of the Kentuckians would hear me on the other side of the river. For that reason I propose to address a portion of what I have to say to the Kentuckians.

I say, then, in the first place, to the Kentuckians, that I am what they call, as I understand it, a "Black Republican." I think Slavery is wrong, morally, and politically. I desire that it should be no further spread in these United States, and I should not object if it should gradually terminate in the whole Union. While I say this for myself, I say to you, Kentuckians, that I understand you differ radically with me upon this proposition; that you believe Slavery is a good thing; that Slavery is right; that it ought to be extended and perpetuated in this Union. Now, there being this broad difference between us, I do not pretend in addressing myself to you, Kentuckians, to attempt proselyting you; that would be a vain effort. I do not enter upon it . . .

I often hear it intimated that you mean to divide the Union whenever a Republican, or anything like it, is elected President of the United States. Well, then, I want to know what you are going to do with your half of it? Are you going to split the Ohio down through, and push your half off a piece? Or are you going to keep it right alongside of us outrageous fellows? Or are you going to build up a wall some way between your country and ours, by which that moveable property of yours can't come over here any more, to the danger of your losing it? Do you think you can better yourselves on that subject, by leaving us here under no obligation whatever to return those specimens of your moveable property that come hither? You have divided the Union because we would not do right with you as you think, upon that subject; when we cease to be under obligations to do anything for you, how much better off do you think you will be? Will you make war upon us and kill us all? Why, gentlemen, I think you are as gallant and as brave men as live; that you can fight as bravely in a good cause, man for man, as any other people living; that you have shown yourselves capable of this upon various occasions; but, man for man, you are not better than we are, and there are not so many of you as there are of us. You will never make much of a hand at whipping us. If we were fewer in numbers than you, I think that you could whip us; if we were equal it would likely be a drawn battle; but being inferior in numbers, you will make nothing by attempting to master us.[21]

Following are excerpts of typical letters Lincoln wrote during the presidential campaign of 1860 and before he took office, refusing to back down on the extension of slavery.

Let there be no compromise on the question of extending slavery. If there be, all our labor is lost, and ere long, must be done again. The dangerous ground—that into which some of our friends have a hankering to run—is Pop[ular] Sov[ereignty]. Have none of it. Stand firm. The tug has to come, and better now than any time hereafter.[22]

On the territorial question—that is, the question of extending slavery under national auspices—I am inflexible. I am for no compromise which assists or permits the extension of the institution on soil owned by the nation.[23]

But why should any go, who really think slavery ought not to spread? Do they really think the right ought to yield to the wrong? Are they afraid to stand by the right? Do they fear that the constitution is too weak to sustain them in the right? Do they really think that by right surrendering to wrong, the hopes of our constitution, our Union, and our liberties, can possibly be bettered?[24]

In Edwardsville, Illinois Lincoln declared that it was the people's love of liberty, instilled in them by God, that gave the nation hope.

Now, when by all these means you have succeeded in dehumanizing the negro; when you have put him down, and made it forever impossible for him to be but as the beasts of the field; when you have extinguished his soul, and placed him where the ray of hope is blown out in darkness like that which broods over the spirits of the damned; are you quite sure the demon which you have roused will not turn and rend you? What constitutes the bulwark of our own liberty and independence? It is not our frowning battlements, our bristling sea coasts, the guns of our war steamers, or the strength of our gallant and disciplined army. These are not our reliance against a resumption of tyranny in our fair land. All of them may be turned against our liberties, without making us stronger or weaker for the struggle. Our reliance is in the love of liberty which God has planted in our bosoms. Our defense is in the preservation of the spirit which prizes liberty as the heritage of all men, in all lands, every where. Destroy this spirit, and you have planted the seeds of despotism around your own doors. Familiarize yourselves with the chains of bondage, and you are preparing your own limbs to wear them. Accustomed to trample on the rights of those around you, you have lost the genius of your own independence, and become the fit subjects of the first cunning tyrant who rises. And let me tell you, all these things are prepared for you with the logic of history, if the elections shall promise that the next Dred Scott decision and all future decisions will be quietly acquiesced in by the people.[25]

In Peoria, Illinois Lincoln berated Douglas for minimizing the importance of the slavery issue and diminishing the black man's status to subhuman.

In the course of his reply, Senator Douglas remarked, in substance, that he had always considered this government was made for the white people and not for the negroes. Why, in point of mere fact, I think so too. But in this remark of the Judge, there is a significance, which I think is the key to the great mistake (if there is any such mistake) which he has made in this Nebraska measure. It shows that the Judge has no very vivid impression that the negro is a human; and consequently has no idea that there can be any moral question in legislating about him. In his view, the question of whether a new country shall be slave or free, is a matter of as utter indifference, as it is whether his neighbor shall plant his farm with tobacco, or stock it with horned cattle. Now, whether this view is right or wrong, it is very certain that the great mass of mankind take a totally different view. They consider slavery a great moral wrong; and their feelings against it, is not evanescent, but eternal. It lies at the very foundation of their sense of justice; and it cannot be trifled with. It is a great and durable element of popular action, and, I think, no statesman can safely disregard it.[26]

Lincoln's debates with Douglas brought him political fame and he was invited to speak to an influential Republican audience at the Cooper Union in New York City in February 1860. Never an impressive figure at first sight, his enthusiasm for his subject and meticulous research transformed the audience from a skeptical group of listeners to a cheering crowd. He closed with the following words.

Holding, as [Southerners] do, that slavery is morally right, and socially elevating, they cannot cease to demand a full national recognition of it, as a legal right, and a social blessing.

Nor can we justifiably withhold this, on any ground save our conviction that slavery is wrong. If slavery is right, all words, acts, laws, and constitutions against it, are themselves wrong, and should be silenced, and swept away. If it is right, we cannot justly object to its nationality—its universality; if it is wrong, they cannot justly insist upon its extension—its enlargement. All they ask, we could readily grant, if we thought slavery right; all we ask, they could as readily grant, if they thought it wrong. Their thinking it right, and our thinking it wrong, is the precise fact upon which depends the whole controversy. Thinking it right, as they do, they are not to blame for desiring its full recognition, as being right; but, thinking it wrong, as we do, can we yield to them? Can we cast our votes with their view, and against our own? In view of our moral, social, and political responsibilities, can we do this?

Wrong as we think slavery is, we can yet afford to let it alone where it is, because that much is due to the necessity arising from its actual presence in the nation; but can we, while our votes will prevent it, allow it to spread into the national Territories and to overrun us here in these free States?

If our sense of duty forbids this, then let us stand by our duty fearlessly and effectively. Let us be diverted by none of those sophistical contrivances wherewith we are so industriously plied and belabored—contrivances such as groping for some middle ground between the right and the wrong; vain as the search for a man who should be neither a living man nor a dead man; such as a policy of "don't care" on a question about which all true men do care; such as Union appeals beseeching true Union men to yield to Disunionists, reversing the divine rule, and calling, not the sinners, but the righteous to repentance; such as invocations to Washington, imploring men to unsay what Washington said and undo what Washington did.

Neither let us be slandered from our duty by false accusations against us, nor frightened from it by menaces of destruction to the government, nor of dungeons to ourselves. Let us have faith that right makes might; and in that faith let us to the end dare to do our duty as we understand it.[27]

In this letter to a political confidant a few months before the Republican Presidential Convention, Lincoln revealed part of his political strategy for taking the nomination away from Seward and his other rivals.

My name is new in the field, and I suppose I am not the first choice of a very great many. Our policy, then, is to give no offense to others—leave them in a mood to come to us if they shall be compelled to give up their first love. This, too, is dealing justly with all, and leaving us in a mood to support heartily whoever shall be nominated.[28]

In the following, Lincoln displayed his contempt for those that support slavery.

I have always thought that all men should be free; but if any should be slaves it should be first those who desire it for themselves, and secondly those who desire it for others. Whenever [I] hear any one, arguing for slavery I feel a strong impulse to see it tried on him personally.[29]

Lincoln expressed frustration over the different way the supporters and opponents of slavery defined the term "liberty."

The world has never had a good definition of the word liberty, and the American people, just now, are much in want of one. We all declare for liberty; but in using the same word we do not all mean the same thing. With some the word liberty may mean for each man to do as he pleases with himself, and the product of his labor; while with others the same word may mean for some men to do as they please with other men, and the product of other men's labor. Here are two, not only different, but incompatable things, called by the same name—liberty. And it follows that each of the things is, by the respective parties, called by two different and incompatable names—liberty and tyranny.

The shepherd drives the wolf from the sheep's throat, for which the sheep thanks the shepherd as a liberator, while the wolf denounces him for the same act as the destroyer of liberty, especially as the sheep was a black one. Plainly the sheep and the wolf are not agreed upon a definition of the word liberty; and precisely the same difference prevails to-day among us human creatures, even in the North, and all professing to love liberty. Hence we behold the processes by which thousands are daily passing from under the yoke of bondage, hailed by some as the advance of liberty, and bewailed by others as the destruction of all liberty. Recently, as it seems, the people of Maryland have been doing something to define liberty; and thanks to them that, in what they have done, the wolf's dictionary, has been repudiated.[30]

Soon after Lincoln's election Southern states began seceding from the Union. While boarding the train that would take him to Washington, D.C., Lincoln demonstrated increasing trust in God in his famous farewell speech to the people of Springfield.

Presidential candidate Abraham Lincoln, taken in August 1860. Lincoln did not grow a beard until shortly before taking office in early 1861.

Library of Congress

My friends: No one, not in my situation, can appreciate my feeling of sadness at this parting. To this place, and the kindness of these people, I owe everything. Here I have lived a quarter of a century, and have passed from a young to an old man. Here my children have been born, and one is buried. I now leave, not knowing when or whether ever I may return, with a task before me greater than that which rested upon Washington. Without the assistance of that Divine Being who ever attended him, I cannot succeed. With that assistance, I cannot fail. Trusting in Him who can go with me, and remain with you, and be everywhere for good, let us confidently hope that all will yet be well. To His care commending you, as I hope in your prayers you will commend me, I bid you an affectionate farewell.[31]

Chapter 7

Presidential Leadership

Lincoln was ill-prepared for the presidency when he took office. He had no formal education or administrative training, very little military experience, and had served only a single term in Congress. Even though he had none of these advantages, he demonstrated several leadership skills that proved essential to his effectiveness during the Civil War. First of all, he clearly defined his primary goal, maintenance of the Union, and never lost sight of it. Secondly, he used his superior communication skills to keep the people focused on the main goal. Finally, he maintained an unshakable trust that if he would only follow God's direction, the Almighty would save the country and democratic government. The following letters and speeches illustrate these and other leadership qualities of Lincoln.

Long before he became president, Lincoln demonstrated one of his well-known qualities, commitment to principle, in this simple statement.

The probability that we may fail in the struggle ought not to deter us from the support of a cause we believe to be just.[1]

Although most of Lincoln's First Inaugural was dedicated to placating the South, he ended the address with both a plea for friendship and a thinly veiled threat.

In your hands, my dissatisfied fellow-countrymen, and not in mine, is the momentous issue of civil war. The government will not assail you. You can have no conflict without being yourselves the aggressors. You have no oath registered in heaven to destroy the government, while I shall have the most solemn one to "preserve, protect, and defend it."

I am loath to close. We are not enemies, but friends. We must not be enemies. Though passion may have strained, it must not break our bonds of affection. The mystic chords of memory, stretching from every battlefield and patriot grave to every living heart and hearthstone all over this broad land, will yet swell the chorus of the Union when again touched, as surely they will be, by the better angels of our nature.[2]

In his first address to Congress, the following of which are the closing lines, he described his reason for responding to the attack on Fort Sumter and prosecuting the war.

Our popular government has often been called an experiment. Two points in it our people have already settled—the successful establishing and the successful administering of it. One still remains—its successful maintenance against a formidable internal attempt to overthrow it. It is now for them to demonstrate to the world that those who can fairly carry an election can also suppress a rebellion; that ballots are the rightful and peaceful successors of bullets; and that when ballots have fairly and constitutionally decided, there can be no successful appeal back to bullets; that there can be no successful appeal, except to ballots themselves, at succeeding elections. Such will be a great lesson of peace: teaching men that what they cannot take by an election, neither can they take it by a war; teaching all the folly of being the beginners of a war.

Lest there be some uneasiness in the minds of candid men as to what is to be the course of the government toward the Southern States after the rebellion shall have been suppressed, the executive deems it proper to say it will be his purpose then, as ever, to be guided by the Constitution and the laws; and that he probably will have no different understanding of the powers and duties of the Federal Government relatively to the rights of the States and the people, under the Constitution, than that expressed in the inaugural address.

He desires to preserve the government, that it may be administered for all as it was administered by the men who made it. Loyal citizens everywhere have the right to claim this their government, and the government has no right to withhold or neglect it. It is not perceived that in giving it there is any coercion, any conquest, or any subjugation, in any just sense of those terms.

The Constitution provides, and all the States have accepted the provision, that "the United States shall guarantee to every State in this Union a republican form of government." But if a State may lawfully go out of the Union, having done so, it may also discard the republican form of government; so that to prevent its going out is an indispensable means to the end of maintaining the guarantee mentioned; and when an end is lawful and obligatory, the indispensable means to it are also lawful and obligatory.

It was with the deepest regret that the executive found the duty of employing the war power in defense of the government forced upon him. He could but perform this duty or surrender the existence of the government.

No compromise by public servants could, in this case, be a cure; not that compromises are not often proper, but that no popular government can long survive a marked precedent that those who carry an election can only save the government from immediate destruction by giving up the main point upon which the people gave the election. The people themselves, and not their servants, can safely reverse their own deliberate decisions.

As a private citizen the executive could not have consented that these institutions shall perish; much less could he, in betrayal of so vast and so sacred a trust as the free people have confided to him. He felt that he had no moral right to shrink, nor even to count the chances of his own life in what might follow. In full view of his great responsibility he has, so far, done what he has deemed his duty. You will now, according to your own judgment, perform yours.

He sincerely hopes that your views and your actions may so accord with his, as to assure all faithful citizens who have been disturbed in their rights of a certain and speedy restoration to them, under the Constitution and the laws.

And having thus chosen our course, without guile and with pure purpose, let us renew our trust in God, and go forward without fear and with manly hearts.[3]

Lincoln demonstrated a characteristic of a great leader when he clearly communicated his primary goal as president.

I am decided; my course is fixed; my path is blazed. The Union and the Constitution shall be preserved and the laws enforced at every and at all hazards. I expect the people to sustain me. They have never yet forsaken any true man.[4]

Lincoln had previously stated that he would "hold McClellan's horse" [5] *if he would only provide the North military victories. But in this April 1862 letter to the general, he demonstrated his patience was wearing thin and he expected decisive action of General McClellan.*

And once more let me tell you it is indispensable to you that you strike a blow. I am powerless to help this. You will do me the justice to remember I always insisted that going down the bay in search of a field, instead of fighting at or near Manassas, was only shifting and not surmounting a difficulty; that we would find the same enemy and the same or equal entrenchments at either place. The country will not fail to note—is noting now—that the present hesitation to move upon an entrenched enemy is but the story of Manassas repeated.

I beg to assure you that I have never written you or spoken to you in greater kindness of feeling than now, nor with a fuller purpose to sustain you, so far as in my most anxious judgment consistently can; but you must act.[6]

In this excerpt from a message to Secretary of State Seward, written in the middle of the Seven Days Battles, Lincoln demonstrated the resolve of a leader that planned to save the Union irregardless of personal cost.

I expect to maintain this contest until successful, or till I die, or am conquered, or my term expires, or Congress or the country forsakes me;[7]

In July of 1862, in a letter to Cuthbert Bullitt, a loyal Union man living in the recently conquered city of New Orleans, Lincoln demonstrated both his commitment to saving the Union and his personal philosophy of dealing with people in a patient, forgiving manner.

I am in no boastful mood. I shall not do more than I can, and I shall do all I can to save the government, which is my sworn duty as well as my personal inclination. I shall do nothing in malice. What I deal with is too vast for malicious dealing.[8]

In this, one of Lincoln's most famous letters, he demonstrated both his commitment to saving the Union and willingness to adopt any measure to accomplish this goal. Lincoln had made the decision, as yet unannounced, to emancipate all slaves residing within those areas under control of the rebelling states, and was waiting for a military victory to publicize it. Noteworthy in this letter are three things. First is the clear statement of his primary goal as president. Second, he observed that the elimination of slavery, although of lesser importance when compared to saving the Union, may be key to the attainment of the primary goal. Finally, he stated that although his own desire was that all men should be free, he did not believe his personal feelings should dictate his duties as president.

The letter was in response to an editorial, published two days before, in the New York Tribune, *entitled "The Prayer of Twenty Millions." In this communication Horace Greeley, editor of the* Tribune, *had lectured Lincoln on the need to execute the confiscation acts and emancipate the slaves as quickly as possible. Lincoln sent this response to Greeley, hoping for its immediate publication. Greeley complied and published it on August 25, 1862. After a brief introduction, in which Lincoln dismissed Greeley's "dictatorial tone" out of his belief that Greeley was an old friend whose "heart I have always supposed to be right," he continued.*

I would save the Union. I would save it the shortest way under the Constitution. The sooner the national authority can be restored, the nearer the Union will be "the Union as it was." If there be those who would not save the Union unless they could at the same time save slavery, I do not agree with them. If there be those who would not save the Union unless they could at the same time destroy slavery, I do not agree with them.

My paramount object in this struggle is to save the Union, and is not either to save or to destroy slavery. If I could save the Union without freeing any slave, I would do it; and if I could save it by freeing all the slaves, I would do it; and if I could save it by freeing some and leaving others alone, I would also do that. What I do about slavery and the colored race, I do because I believe it helps to save the Union; and what I forbear, I forbear because I do not believe it would help to save the Union. I shall do less whenever I shall believe what I am doing hurts the cause, and I shall do more whenever I shall believe doing more will help the cause. I shall try to correct errors when shown to be errors, and I shall adopt new views so fast as they shall appear to be true views.

I have here stated my purpose according to my view of official duty; and I intend no modification of my oft-expressed personal wish that all men everywhere could be free.[9]

A few days after the Battle of Antietam Lincoln issued his announcement that as of January 1, 1863, the South's slaves would be free. This is an excerpt from the preliminary Emancipation Proclamation.

On the first day of January, in the year of our Lord one thousand eight hundred and sixty-three, all persons held as slaves within any State or designated part of a State the people whereof shall then be in rebellion against the United States, shall be then, thenceforward, and forever free; and the Executive Government of the United States, including the military and naval authority thereof, will recognize and maintain the freedom of such persons, and will do no act or acts to repress such persons, or any of them, in any efforts they may make for their actual freedom.[10]

The Republican Party suffered badly during the 1862 congressional elections and lost several seats in Congress. Whether this was mostly due to people's disappointment with Lincoln's decision to free the slaves, their frustration over the way the war was being conducted, or that the soldiers, the most ardent supporters of Lincoln, were unable to vote, is a matter of some debate.[11] In the following, Lincoln responded to General Carl Schurz, an officer who had been appointed to that rank because of his political connections. Schurz had previously sent Lincoln a letter that had criticized the president's leadership skills. The response dated November 24, 1862, is a classic combination of wit and sarcasm.

My dear Sir:

I have just received and read your letter of the 20th. The purport of it is that we lost the late elections and the Administration is failing because the war is unsuccessful, and that I must not flatter myself that I am not justly to blame for it. I certainly know that if the war fails, the Administration fails, and that I will be blamed for it, whether I deserve it or not. And I ought to be blamed if I could do better. You think I could do better; therefore, you blame me already. I think I could not do better; therefore I blame you for blaming me. I understand you now to be willing to accept the help of men who are not Republicans, provided they have "heart in it." Agreed. I want no others. But who is to be the judge of hearts, or of "heart in it?" If I must discard my own judgment and take yours, I must also take that of others; and by the time I should reject all I should be advised to reject, I should have none left, Republicans or other—not even yourself. For be assured, my dear sir, there are men who have "heart in it" that think you are performing your part as poorly as you think I am performing mine.[12]

Lincoln's annual message to Congress on December 1, 1862, was the equivalent to the modern State of the Union Address. In it he reported statistical data on the economy, updates of diverse events such as the Sioux Indian uprising in Minnesota, and announced noteworthy actions such as the recent establishment of the Department of Agriculture. Finally, he closed with one of his most eloquent pleas to Congress, asking that it support his efforts to save the Union and provide freedom for the slaves.

We can succeed only by concert. It is not "Can *any* of us *imagine* better?" but "Can we *all* do better?" The dogmas of the quiet past are inadequate to the stormy present. The occasion is piled high with difficulty, and we must rise with the occasion. As our case is new, so we must think anew and act anew. We must disenthrall ourselves, and then we shall save our country.

Fellow-citizens, we cannot escape history. We of this Congress and this administration will be remembered in spite of ourselves. No personal significance or insignificance can spare one or another of us. The fiery trial through which we pass will light us down, in honor or dishonor, to the latest generation. We say we are for the Union. The world will not forget that we say this. We know how to save the Union. The world knows we do know how to save it. We—even we here—hold the power and bear the responsibility. In giving freedom to the slave, we assure freedom to the free—honorable alike in what we give and what we preserve. We shall nobly save or meanly lose the last, best hope of earth. Other means may succeed; this could not fail. The way is plain, peaceful, generous, just—a way which, if followed, the world will forever applaud, and God must forever bless.[13]

This letter to Major General Joseph Hooker dated January 26, 1863, is a remarkable example of Lincoln's ability to provide candid criticism without offense to the recipient. As a Grand Division commander under General Burnside, Hooker had intrigued with other officers to remove Burnside from the army. Hooker had also stated that what the country really needed was a "dictator," implying that he himself might be the best man for this position. Lincoln ignored this slight and patiently explained what he expected of Hooker now that he has been placed in command.

General:

I have placed you at the head of the Army of the Potomac. Of course I have done this upon what appear to me to be sufficient reasons, and yet I think it best for you to know that there are some things in regard to which I am not quite satisfied with you. I believe you to be a brave and skilful soldier, which of course I like. I also believe you do not mix politics with your profession, in which you are right. You have confidence in yourself, which is a valuable if not an indispensable quality. You are ambitious, which, within reasonable bounds, does good rather than harm; but I think that during General Burnside's command of the army you have taken counsel of your ambition and thwarted him as much as you could, in which you did a great wrong to the country and to a most meritorious and honorable brother officer.

I have heard, in such a way as to believe it, of your recently saying that both the army and the government needed a dictator. Of course it was not for this, but in spite of it, that I have given you the command. Only those generals who gain successes can set up dictators. What I now ask of you is military success, and I will risk the dictatorship.

The government will support you to the utmost of its ability, which is neither more nor less than it has done and will do for all commanders. I much fear that the spirit which you have aided to infuse into the army, of criticizing their commander and withholding confidence from him, will now turn upon you. I shall assist you as far as I can to put it down. Neither you nor Napoleon, if he were alive again, could get any good out of an army while such a spirit prevails in it; and now beware of rashness. Beware of rashness, but with energy and sleepless vigilance go forward and give us victories.[14]

Lincoln exasperated his generals by insisting on reviewing the military court-martial records and sometimes pardoning men condemned to be shot. In discussing his desire to pardon condemned men, he said:

Some of my generals complain that I impair discipline and subordination in the army by my pardons and respites, but it makes me rested, after a day's hard work if I can find some good excuse for saving a man's life, and I go to bed happy as I think how joyous the signing of my name will make him and his family and friends.[15]

In a letter to Erastus Corning on June 12, 1863, Lincoln complained about laws that required him to shoot the soldier that ran away, and yet tied his hands in dealing with the politician that induced desertion.

Long experience has shown that armies cannot be maintained unless desertion shall be punished by the severe penalty of death. The case requires, and the law and the Constitution sanction, this punishment. Must I shoot a simple-minded soldier boy who deserts, while I must not touch a hair of a wily agitator who induces him to desert?[16]

General U. S. Grant took the Confederate stronghold of Vicksburg, Mississippi using the unconventional method of abandoning the countryside and going below the city to attack from the south and east. Lincoln had wanted Grant to unite with another force under General Nathaniel Banks and capture Port Hudson, Louisiana before attacking Vicksburg. But Grant did not do it this way. In the following letter to Grant, dated July 13, 1863, Lincoln demonstrated his willingness to both praise his field commander and admit his own errors.

My dear General:

I do not remember that you and I ever met personally. I write this now as a grateful acknowledgment for the almost inestimable service you have done the country. I wish to say a word further. When you first reached the vicinity of Vicksburg, I thought you should do what you finally did—march the troops across the neck, run the batteries with the transports, and thus go below; and I never had any faith, except a general hope that you knew better than I, that the Yazoo Pass expedition and the like could succeed. When you got below and took Port Gibson, Grand Gulf, and vicinity, I thought you should go down the river and join General Banks, and when you turned northward, east of the Big Black, I feared it was a mistake. I now wish to make the personal acknowledgment that you were right and I was wrong.[17]

In August of 1863, Lincoln provided a letter to an old friend from Springfield discussing his support of black troops. He asked his friend to read it to a political meeting in Springfield, hoping it would engender more support for his policy of enlisting blacks into the army. These are the closing lines.

Peace does not appear so distant as it did. I hope it will come soon, and come to stay; and so come as to be worth the keeping in all future time. It will then have been proved that, among free men, there can be no successful appeal from the ballot to the bullet; and that they who take such appeal are sure to lose their case, and pay the cost. And then, there will be some black men who can remember that, with silent tongue, and clenched teeth, and steady eye, and well-poised bayonet, they have helped mankind on to this great consummation; while, I fear, there will be some white ones, unable to forget that, with malignant heart, and deceitful speech, they have strove to hinder it.

Still let us not be over-sanguine of a speedy final triumph. Let us be quite sober. Let us diligently apply the means, never doubting that a just God, in his own good time, will give us the rightful result.[18]

A few months after the Battle of Gettysburg, Lincoln received an invitation to speak at the dedication ceremony of the cemetery established for the men killed there. In this address, the most famous of all of Lincoln's speeches, he demonstrated transforming leadership skills when he declared it a war dedicated to a "new birth of freedom."

Fourscore and seven years ago our fathers brought forth on this continent a new nation, conceived in liberty, and dedicated to the proposition that all men are created equal.

Now we are engaged in a great civil war, testing whether that nation, or any nation so conceived and so dedicated, can long endure. We are met on a great battle-field of that war. We have come to dedicate a portion of that field as a final resting-place for those who here gave their lives that that nation might live. It is altogether fitting and proper that we should do this.

But, in a larger sense, we cannot dedicate—we cannot consecrate—we cannot hallow—this ground. The brave men, living and dead, who struggled here, have consecrated it far above our poor power to add or detract. The world will little note nor long remember what we say here, but it can never forget what they did here. It is for us, the living, rather, to be dedicated here to the unfinished work which they who fought here have thus far so nobly advanced. It is rather for us to be here dedicated to the great task remaining before us—that from these honored dead we take increased devotion to that cause for which they gave the last full measure of devotion; that we here highly resolve that these dead shall not have died in vain; that this nation,

The famous abolitionist Frederick Douglass, a former slave who became a friend of Lincoln.

National Archives

under God, shall have a new birth of freedom; and that government of the people, by the people, for the people, shall not perish from the earth.[19]

At a Sanity Fair in Washington, D.C., Lincoln gave a short speech to express his gratitude to both the common soldier for bearing its burdens, and to the women of America, who had faithfully sustained the war effort.

Ladies and Gentlemen: I appear to say but a word. This extra-ordinary war in which we are engaged falls heavily upon all classes of people, but the most heavily upon the soldier. For it has been said, all that a man hath will he give for his life; and while all contribute of their substance the soldier puts his life at stake, and often yields it up in his country's cause. The highest merit, then, is due to the soldier.

In this extraordinary war extraordinary developments have manifested themselves, such as have not been seen in former wars; and amongst these manifestations nothing has been more remarkable than these fairs for the relief of suffering soldiers and their families. And the chief agents in these fairs are the women of America.

I am not accustomed to the use of language of eulogy; I have never studied the art of paying compliments to women; but I must say that if all that has been said by orators and poets since the creation of the world in praise of woman were applied to the women of America, it would not do them justice for their conduct during this war. I will close by saying God bless the women of America![20]

Lincoln wrote the following letter dated April 4, 1864, to document something he had said in a previous conversation. He first stated his position that he believed the office of the presidency gave him no right to take a particular action on slavery unless it was essential to saving the Union. Next he explained his intention to take whatever measures he perceived necessary to save the Union, including a liberal interpretation of his executive powers in the Constitution. What he had in mind primarily was the suspension of habeas corpus, something he did many times during the war.

My dear Sir:

You ask me to put in writing the substance of what I verbally said the other day in your presence, to Governor Bramlette and Senator Dixon. It was about as follows.

"I am naturally antislavery. If slavery is not wrong, nothing is wrong. I cannot remember when I did not so think and feel, and yet I have never understood that the presidency conferred upon me an unrestricted right to act officially upon this judgment and feeling. It was in the oath I took that I would, to the best of my ability, preserve, protect, and defend the Constitution of the United States. I could not take the office without taking the oath. Nor was it my view that I might take an oath to get power, and break the oath in using the power.

I understood, too, that in ordinary civil administration this oath even forbade me to practically indulge my primary abstract judgment on the moral question of slavery. I had publicly declared this many times, and in many ways. And I aver that, to this day, I have done no official act in mere deference to my abstract judgment and feeling on slavery.

I did understand, however, that my oath to preserve the Constitution to the best of my ability imposed upon me the duty of preserving, by every indispensable means, that government—that nation, of which that Constitution was the organic law. Was it possible to lose the nation and yet preserve the Constitution? By general law, life and limb must be protected, yet often a limb must be amputated to save a life; but a life is never wisely given to save a limb. I felt that measures otherwise unconstitutional might become lawful by becoming indispensable to the preservation of the Constitution through the preservation of the nation. Right or wrong, I assume this ground, and now avow it. I could not feel that, to the best of my ability, I had even tried to preserve the Constitution, if, to save slavery or any minor matter, I should permit the wreck of government, country, and Constitution all together. . . ."

I add a word which was not in the verbal conversation. In telling this tale I attempt no compliment to my own sagacity. I claim not to have controlled events, but confess plainly that events have controlled me. Now, at the end of three years' struggle, the nation's condition is not what either party, or any man, devised or expected. God alone can claim it. Whither it is tending seems plain. If God now wills the removal of a great wrong, and wills also that we of the North, as well as you of the South, shall pay fairly for our complicity in that wrong, impartial history will find therein new cause to attest and revere the justice and goodness of God.[21]

Lincoln explained his justification and timing for freeing the slaves to an artist that lived in the White House for six months. Although this is an excellent synopsis of the practical reasons he freed the slaves, it does not address the moral reasons.

Mr. Thompson, the people of Great Britain, and of other foreign governments, were in one great error in reference to this conflict. They seemed to think that, the moment I was President, I had the power to abolish slavery, forgetting that, before I could have any power whatever, I had to take the oath to support the Constitution of the United States, and execute the laws as I found them. When the Rebellion broke out, my duty did not admit of a question. That was, first, by all strictly lawful means to endeavor to maintain the integrity of the government, I did not consider that I had a right to touch the "State" institution of "Slavery" until all other measures for restoring the Union had failed. The paramount idea of the constitution is the preservation of the Union. It may not be specified in so many words, but that this was the idea of its founders is evident; for, whithout the Union, the constitution would be worthless. It seems clear, then, that in the last extremity, if any local institution threatened the existence of the Union, the Executive could not hesitate as to his duty. In our case, the moment came when I felt that slavery must die that the nation might live! I have sometimes used the illustration in this connection of a man with a diseased limb, and his surgeon. So long as there is a chance of the patient's restoration, the surgeon is solemnly bound to try to save both life and limb; but when the crisis comes, and the limb must be sacrificed as the only chance of saving the life, no honest man will hesitate.

Many of my strongest supporters urged Emancipation before I thought it indispensable, and, I may say, before I thought the country ready for it. It is my conviction that, had the proclamation been issued even six months earlier than it was, public sentiment would not have sustained it.[22]

In the following excerpt from the 1864 annual message to Congress, Lincoln proudly announced that although the nation had been engaged in a bitter Civil War, the North was stronger than ever. He also implied that he would resign the presidency if there were any attempt by the people to return the slaves to slavery.

The important fact remains demonstrated that we have more men now than we had when the war began; that we are not exhausted, nor in process of exhaustion; that we are gaining strength, and may, if need be, maintain the contest indefinitely. This as to men. Material resources are now more complete and abundant than ever.

The national resources, then, are unexhausted, and, as we believe, inexhaustible. The public purpose to re-establish and maintain the national authority is unchanged, and, as we believe, unchangeable. . . . In presenting the abandonment of armed resistance to the national authority on the part of the insurgents as the only indispensable condition to ending the war on the part of the government, I retract nothing heretofore said as to slavery. I repeat the declaration made a year ago, that "while I remain in my present position I shall not attempt to retract or modify the Emancipation Proclamation, nor shall I return to slavery any person who is free by the terms of that proclamation, or by any of the acts of Congress."

If the people should, by whatever mode or means, make it an executive duty to re-enslave such persons, another, and not I, must be their instrument to perform it.

In stating a single condition of peace, I mean simply to say, that the war will cease on the part of the government whenever it shall have ceased on the part of those who began it.[23]

In the following, Lincoln expressed hope that the people would sustain his efforts to prosecute the war to a successful end.

I am struggling to maintain government, not to overthrow it. I am struggling especially to prevent others from overthrowing it. I therefore say, that if I shall live, I shall remain President until the fourth of next March; and that whoever shall be constitutionally elected therefore in November, shall be duly installed as President on the fourth of March; and that in the interval I shall do my utmost that whoever is to hold the helm for the next voyage, shall start with the best possible chance to save the ship.

This is due to the people both on principle, and under the constitution. Their will, constitutionally expressed, is the ultimate law for all. If they should deliberately resolve to have immediate peace even at the loss of their country, and their liberty, I know not the power or the right to resist them. It is their own business, and they must do as they please with their own. I believe, however, they are still resolved to preserve their country and their liberty; and in this, in office or out of it, I am resolved to stand by them.

I may add that in this purpose to save the country and its liberties, no classes of people seem so nearly unanimous as the soldiers in the field and the seamen afloat. Do they not have the hardest of it? Who should quail while they do not?

God bless the soldiers and seamen, with all their brave commanders.[24]

One of the quaint traditions of the Civil War era was the serenade, where people would gather on the White House lawn and pay tribute to the president. Lincoln frequently responded to these with a short speech, sometimes prepared in advance, for the dual purpose of saying thanks and providing some sort of policy statement. The following is a response Lincoln made to a serenade on November 8, 1864, shortly after his successful reelection to the presidency.

I am thankful to God for this approval of the people; but, while deeply grateful for this mark of their confidence in me, if I know my heart, my gratitude is free from any taint of personal triumph. I do not impugn the motives of anyone opposed to me. It is no pleasure to me to triumph over any one, but I give thanks to the Almighty for this evidence of the people's resolution to stand by free government and the rights of humanity.[25]

Chapter 8
Faith in God

Lincoln was raised by Christian parents that taught him to revere God and respect the Bible as Divine revelation. But when he went out on his own as a young man, he apparently developed a sense of abandonment by God and became skeptical of Christianity. As he matured, and experienced hardships such as the death of two children and the war, his faith increased until he was again seeking God in prayer and by reading the Bible. Lincoln finally accepted that Jesus Christ was "the Saviour" of mankind, but whether or not Christ became his personal Savior is a debatable question. There is no tangible evidence or corroborative historical testimony to indicate that he actually became a Christian. Even though he supposedly went through a period of skepticism, none of his surviving letters or speeches manifest anything but belief in God and a genuine respect for the Bible.

At the age of 22, Lincoln moved to New Salem, Illinois, a small community with various Christian denominations. Each church had a creed or statement of faith that had to be accepted before an individual could join. Lincoln saw these creeds as unnecessary, and was appalled at the rivalry between the community's different church groups. He stated his reason for never joining a church.

I have never united myself to any church, because I have found difficulty in giving my assent, without mental reservation, to the long, complicated statements of Christian doctrine which characterize their Articles of Belief and Confessions of Faith. When any church will inscribe over its altar, as its sole qualification for membership, the Saviour's condensed statement of the substance of both Law and Gospel, "Thou shalt love the Lord thy God with all thy heart, and with all thy soul, and with all thy mind, and thy neighbor as thyself," that church will I join with all my heart and all my soul.[1]

During Lincoln's campaign for Congress in 1846, his political antagonists used the fact he was not a member of any church against him, and spread rumors that he was a "free thinker" in his beliefs. In a handbill he had produced for the campaign, Lincoln stated:

That I am not a member of any Christian church is true; but I have never denied the truth of the Scriptures; and I have never spoken with intentional disrespect of religion in general, or of any denomination of Christians in particular. It is true that in early life I was inclined to believe in what I understand is called the "Doctrine of Necessity"—that is, that the human mind is impelled to action, or held in rest by some power, over which the mind itself has no control; and I have sometimes (with one, two, or three, but never publicly) tried to maintain this opinion in argument. The habit of arguing thus however, I have entirely left off for more than five years. And I add here, I have always understood this same opinion to be held by several of the Christian denominations. The foregoing, is the whole truth, briefly stated, in relation to myself, upon this subject.

I do not think I could myself be brought to support a man for office whom I knew to be an open enemy of, or scoffer at, religion. Leaving the higher matter of eternal consequences, between him and his Maker, I still do not think any man has the right thus to insult the feelings, and injure the morals, of the community in which he may live. If, then, I was guilty of such conduct, I should blame no man who should condemn me for it; but I do blame those whoever they may be, who falsely put such a charge in circulation against me.[2]

During the Lincoln-Douglas debates, Lincoln began to articulate more clearly his maturing faith and belief that God was intervening in the nation's events. While listening to Lincoln, Douglas sometimes felt the sting of his adversary's political wit, as well as biblical knowledge.

My friend [Douglas] has said to me that I am a poor hand to quote Scripture. I will try it again, however. It is said in one of the admonitions of our Lord, "Be ye [therefore] perfect even as your Father which is in heaven is perfect." The Saviour, I suppose, did not expect that any human creature could be perfect as the Father in heaven; but he said, "As your father in heaven is perfect, be ye also perfect." He set that up as a standard, and he who did most toward reaching that standard attained the highest degree of moral perfection. So I say in relation to the principle that all men are created equal, let it be as nearly reached as we can. If we cannot give freedom to every creature, let us do nothing that will impose slavery upon any other creature. Let us then turn this government back into the channel in which the framers of the Constitution originally placed it. Let us stand firmly by each other. If we do not do so, we are tending in the contrary direction that our friend Judge Douglas proposes—not intentionally—working in the traces that tend to make this one universal slave nation. He is one that runs in that direction, and as such I resist him.[3]

Lincoln expressed both faith and frustration in attempting to determine God's will.

There is no contending against the Will of God; but still there is some difficulty in ascertaining, and applying it, to particular cases.[4]

Although Lincoln lost the Senate election to Douglas, he demonstrated he had no hard feelings when he said:

I can only say that I have acted upon my best convictions, without selfishness or malice, and that by the help of God I shall continue to do so.[5]

Lincoln was inaugurated president on March 4, 1861. His First Inaugural Address was primarily an attempt to convince the Southern people that his election was no cause for rebellion. With his best effort at logical argument taking up the largest part of the address, he finally closed with this appeal to the Southern people's sense of community with the North.

My countrymen, one and all, think calmly and well upon this whole subject. Nothing valuable can be lost by taking time. If there be an object to hurry any of you in hot haste to a step which you would never take deliberately, that object will be frustrated by taking time; but no good object can be frustrated by it. Such of you as are now dissatisfied, still have the old Constitution unimpaired, and, on the sensitive point, the laws of your own framing under it; while the new administration will have no immediate power, if it would, to change either. If it were admitted that you who are dissatisfied hold the right side in the dispute, there still is no single good reason for precipitate action. Intelligence, patriotism, Christianity, and a firm reliance on Him who has never yet forsaken this favored land are still competent to adjust, in the best way, all our present difficulty.[6]

Lincoln's reaction to the Union's first military defeat at Manassas, Virginia was to bring a new commander, General George B. McClellan, to take charge of the North's principle eastern army. He then responded to a request from Congress and announced his first national call to prayer.

Excerpt from Proclamation of National Fast Day, August 12, 1861:
[W]hereas it is fit and becoming in all people, at all times, to acknowledge and revere the supreme Government of God; to bow in humble

submission to his chastisements; to confess and deplore their sins and transgressions, in the full conviction that the fear of the Lord is the beginning of wisdom; and to pray with all fervency and contrition, for the pardon of their past offences, and for a blessing upon their present and prospective action:

And whereas when our own beloved country, once, by the blessing of God, united, prosperous and happy, is now afflicted with faction and civil war, it is peculiarly fit for us to recognize the hand of God in this terrible visitation, and in sorrowful rememberance of our own faults and crimes as a nation and as individuals, to humble ourselves before him, and to pray for his mercy—to pray that we may be spared further punishment, though most justly deserved; that our arms may be blessed and made effectual for the re-establishment of law, order, and peace, throughout the wide extent of our country; and that the inestimable boon of civil and religious liberty, earned under his guidance and blessing, by the labors and sufferings of our fathers, may be restored in all its original excellence:

Therefore I, Abraham Lincoln, President of the United States, do appoint the last Thursday in September next as a day of humiliation, prayer, and fasting for all the people of the nation. And I do earnestly recommend to all the people, and especially to the ministers and teachers of religion, of all denominations, and to the heads of families, to observe and keep the day, according to their several creeds and modes of worship, in all humility and with all religious solemnity, to the end that the united prayer of the nation may ascend to the Throne of Grace and bring down plentiful blessings upon our country.[7]

Lincoln expressed his sense of personal inadequacy to Governor Lot M. Morrill of Maine sometime shortly after taking office as president.

I don't know but that God has created some one man great enough to comprehend the whole of this stupendous crisis and transaction from beginning to end, and endowed him with sufficient wisdom to manage and direct it. I confess I do not fully understand, and foresee it all. But I am placed here where I am obliged to the best of my poor ability to deal with it. And that being the case I can only go just as fast as I can see how to go.[8]

Lincoln was acutely aware that as president in the middle of a bitter Civil War, he had to put his own feelings aside and unite the people behind him. Taking to heart the teachings of Christ, he ignored the insults and selfish actions of others and did his best to propagate harmony and concerted action for the Union. The following note is typical of what he would insert in private correspondence, hoping to engender a similar attitude in the reader.

I am a patient man—always willing to forgive on the Christian terms of repentance; and also to give ample time for repentance. Still I must save the government if possible. What I cannot do, of course I will not do; but it may as well be understood, once for all, that I shall not surrender this game [saving the Union] leaving any available card unplayed.[9]

On the day the Union army lost the battle of Second Manassas, Lincoln demonstrated his belief in the sovereignty of God.

The will of God prevails. In great contests each party claims to act in accordance with the will of God. Both may be, and one must be, wrong. God cannot be for and against the same thing at the same time. In the present civil war it is quite possible that God's purpose is something different from the purpose of either party; and yet the human instrumentalities, working just as they do, are of the best adaptation to effect his purpose. I am almost ready to say that this is probably true; that God wills this contest, and wills that it shall not end yet.[10]

On October 26, 1862, Lincoln wrote a reply to Eliza P. Gurney, a Quaker woman that had prayed with him for guidance. Noteworthy is Lincoln's humility and increasing recognition of God's sovereignty of purpose.

I am glad of this interview, and glad to know that I have your sympathy and prayers. We are indeed going through a trial—a fiery trial. In the very responsible position in which I happen to be placed, being a humble instrument in the hands of our Heavenly Father, as I am, and as we all are, to work out his great purposes, I have desired that all my works and acts may be according to his will, and that it might be so, I have sought his aid—but if after endeavoring to do my best in the light which he affords me, I find my efforts fail, I must believe that for some purpose unknown to me, he wills it otherwise. If I had had my way, this war would never have been commenced; if I had been allowed my way this war would have been ended before this, but we find it still continues; and we must believe that he permits it for some wise purpose of his own, mysterious and unknown to us; and though with our limited understandings we may not be able to comprehend it, yet we cannot but believe, that he who made the world still governs it.[11]

On January 5, 1863, Lincoln sent a response to Caleb Russell and Sallie Fenton, members of The Religious Society of Friends (Quakers), who had previously sent him a letter of encouragement. In their letter the Friends had mentioned their approval of the Emancipation Proclamation and the fact that they were praying for him.

It is most cheering and encouraging for me to know that in the efforts which I have made and am making for the restoration of a righteous peace to our country, I am upheld and sustained by the good wishes and prayers of God's people. No one is more deeply than myself aware that without His favor our highest wisdom is but as foolishness and that our most strenuous efforts would avail nothing in the shadow of His displeasure. I am conscious of no desire for my country's welfare that is not in consonance with His will, and of no plan upon which we may not ask His blessing. It seems to me that if there be one subject upon which all good men may unitedly agree, it is imploring the gracious favor of God of Nations upon the struggles our people are making for the preservation of their precious birth-right of civil and religious liberty.[12]

With the Emancipation Proclamation in effect and the spring military campaign against the South about to begin, Lincoln offered one of his most inspiring calls to prayer and fasting.

Proclamation Appointing a National Fast Day March 30, 1863:

[I]t is the duty of nations as well as of men to own their dependence upon the overruling power of God; to confess their sins and transgressions in humble sorrow, yet with assured hope that genuine repentance will lead to mercy and pardon; and to recognize the sublime truth, announced in the Holy Scriptures and proven by all history, that those nations only are blessed whose God is the Lord:

And insomuch as we know that by his divine law nations, like individuals, are subjected to punishments and chastisement in this world, may we not justly fear that the awful calamity of civil war which now desolates the land may be but a punishment inflicted upon us for our presumptuous sins, to the needful end of our national reformation as a whole people?

We have been the recipients of the choicest bounties of Heaven. We have been preserved, these many years, in peace and prosperity. We have grown in numbers, wealth and power as no other nation has ever grown; but we have forgotten God. We have forgotten the gracious hand which preserved us in peace, and multiplied and enriched and strengthened us; and we have vainly imagined, in the deceitfulness of our hearts, that all these blessings were produced by some superior wisdom and virtue of our own. Intoxicated with unbroken success, we have become too self-sufficient to feel the necessity of redeeming and preserving grace, too proud to pray to the God that made us.

It behooves us, then, to humble ourselves before the offended Power, to confess our national sins, and to pray for clemency and forgiveness.

Now, therefore, in compliance with the request, and fully concurring in the views of the Senate, I do by this my proclamation designate and set apart Thursday, the 30th day of April, 1863, as a day of national humiliation, fasting, and prayer. And I do hereby request all the people to abstain, on that day, from their ordinary secular pursuits, and to unite at their several places of public worship and their respective homes in keeping the day holy to the Lord, and devoted to the humble discharge of the religious duties proper to that solemn occasion.

All this being done, in sincerity and truth, let us then rest humbly in the hope authorized by the Divine teachings, that the united cry of the nation will be heard on high, and answered with blessings no less than the pardon of our national sins, and the restoration of our now divided and suffering country to its former happy condition of unity and peace.[13]

In early July 1863, the Union won significant military victories at Gettysburg, Pennsylvania and Vicksburg, Mississippi. Within two weeks of these victories, Lincoln issued the following proclamation of thanksgiving. Noteworthy is Lincoln's statement that the people should invoke the influence of the Holy Spirit to subdue the people's anger and change the hearts of the Southern people.

Proclamation of Thanksgiving: July 15, 1863:

It has pleased Almighty God to hearken to the supplications and prayers of an afflicted people, and to vouchsafe to the army and navy of the United States victories on land and on the sea so signal and so effective as to furnish reasonable grounds for augmented confidence that the union of these States will be maintained, their Constitution preserved, and their peace and prosperity permanently restored. But these victories have been accorded not without sacrifices of life, limb, health, and liberty, incurred by brave, loyal, and patriotic citizens. Domestic affliction in every part of the country follows in the train of these fearful bereavements. It is meet and right to recognize and confess the presence of the Almighty Father, and the power of his hand equally in these triumphs and in these sorrows.

Now, therefore, be it known that I do set apart Thursday, the 6th day of August next, to be observed as a day for national thanksgiving, praise, and prayer, and I invite the people of the United States to assemble on that occasion in their customary places of worship, and, in the forms approved by their own consciences, render the homage due to the Divine Majesty for the wonderful things he has done in the nation's behalf, and invoke the influence of his Holy Spirit to subdue the anger which has produced and so long sustained a needless and cruel rebellion, to change the hearts of the insurgents, to guide the counsels of the government with wisdom adequate to so great a national emergency, and to visit with tender care and consolation throughout the length and breadth of our land all those who, through the vicissitudes of marches, voyages, battles, and sieges have been brought to suffer in mind, body, or estate, and finally to lead the whole nation through the paths of repentance and submission to the Divine Will back to the perfect enjoyment of union and fraternal peace.[14]

Three months after the Battle of Gettysburg, when both armies were back in Virginia and there was no longer any immediate threat to Northern cities, Lincoln again decided to publicly thank God. He issued the following as a proclamation of the first national day of Thanksgiving. This was in response to a request by Sara Josepha Hale, the editor of a popular woman's magazine, Lady's Book. *Prior to this proclamation, the country had no regular national Thanksgiving Day. Some states had an annual Thanksgiving holiday, and there had been sporadic proclamations of national days of Thanksgiving, but Lincoln's proclamation that the "last Thursday in November" be made a national day of thanksgiving became a fixed tradition that presidents repeated for over 75 years.*[15]

Proclamation of Thanksgiving October 3, 1863:

The year that is drawing towards its close has been filled with the blessings of fruitful fields and healthful skies. To these bounties, which are so constantly enjoyed that we are prone to forget the source from which they come, others have been added, which are of so extraordinary a nature that they cannot fail to penetrate and soften the heart which is habitually insensible to the ever watchful providence of Almighty God.

In the midst of a civil war of unequalled magnitude and severity, which has sometimes seemed to foreign states to invite and to provoke their aggression, peace has been preserved with all nations, order has been maintained, the laws have been respected and obeyed, and harmony has prevailed everywhere, except in the theatre of military conflict; while that theatre has been greatly contracted by the advancing armies and navies of the Union.

Needful diversions of wealth and strength from the fields of peaceful industry to the national defence, have not arrested the plow, the shuttle, or the ship; the axe has enlarged the borders of our settlements, and the mines, as well of iron and coal as of the precious metals, have yielded even more abundantly than heretofore. Population has steadily increased, notwithstanding the waste that has been made in the camp, the siege and the battlefield, and the country, rejoicing in the consciousness of augmented strength and vigor, is permitted to expect continuance of years with large increase of freedom.

No human counsel hath devised nor hath any mortal hand worked out these great things. They are the gracious gifts of the Most High God, who, while dealing with us in anger for our sins, hath nevertheless remembered mercy.

It has seemed to me fit and proper that they should be solemnly, reverently, and gratefully acknowledged as with one heart and one voice by the whole American people. I do, therefore, invite my fellow-citizens in every part of the United States, and also those who are at sea and those who are sojourning in foreign lands, to set apart and observe the last Thursday of November next as a day of thanksgiving and praise to our beneficent Father who dwelleth in the heavens. And I recommend to them that, while offering up the ascriptions justly due to Him for such singular deliverances and blessings, they do also, with humble penitence for our national perverseness and disobedience, commend to his tender care all those who have become widows, orphans, mourners or sufferers in the lamentable civil strife in which we are unavoidably engaged, and fervently implore the interposition of the almighty hand to heal the wounds of the nation, and to restore it, as soon as may be consistent with the Divine purposes, to the full enjoyment of peace, harmony, tranquility and Union.[16]

In the following Lincoln succinctly stated his ultimate faith in God.

Amid the greatest difficulties of my Administration, when I could not see any other resort, I would place my whole reliance in God, knowing that all would go well, and that He would decide for the right.[17]

Lincoln again demonstrated his belief that he should follow God's will.

If we do right God will be with us, and if God is with us we cannot fail.[18]

In a September 1864 letter to Eliza P. Guerney, Lincoln again admitted his trust in the wisdom of God.

I have not forgotten—probably never shall forget—the very impressive occasion when yourself and friends visited me on a Sabbath forenoon two years ago. Nor has your kind letter, written nearly a year later, ever been forgotten. In all it has been your purpose to strengthen my reliance on God. I am much indebted to the good Christian people of the country for their constant prayers and consolations; and to no one of them more than to yourself.

The purposes of the Almighty are perfect, and must prevail, though we erring mortals may fail to accurately perceive them in advance. We hoped for a happy termination of this terrible war long before this; but God knows best, and has ruled otherwise. We shall yet acknowledge his wisdom, and our own error therein. Meanwhile we must work earnestly in the best lights he gives us, trusting that so working still conduces to the great ends he ordains. Surely he intends some great good to follow this mighty convulsion, which no mortal could make, and no mortal could stay.

Your people, the Friends, have had, and are having, a very great trial. On principle and faith opposed to both war and oppression, they can only practically oppose oppression by war. In this hard dilemma some have chosen one horn, and some the other. For those appealing to me on conscientious grounds, I have done, and shall do, the best I could and can, in my own conscience, under my oath to the law. That you believe this I doubt not; and, believing it, I shall still receive for our country and myself your earnest prayers to our Father in heaven.[19]

During the course of thanking a group of "loyal colored people of Baltimore" for a Bible they had given him, Lincoln revealed the trust he had in it.

In regard to this Great Book [the Bible], I have but to say, it is the best gift God has given to man. All the good the Saviour gave to the world was communicated through this book. But for it we could not know right from wrong. All things most desirable for man's welfare, here and hereafter, are to be found portrayed in it.[20]

In the summer of 1864, Lincoln had been concerned he would lose the presidential election to McClellan, who was pledged to negotiate a peace with the Confederacy if he won the election. By October of 1864, it was becoming more certain that Lincoln was going to win the presidential election, and the war would be prosecuted to a successful conclusion. This was Lincoln's second annual proclamation of national Thanksgiving.

Proclamation of Thanksgiving October 20, 1864:
It has pleased Almighty God to prolong our national life another year, defending us with his guardian care against unfriendly designs from abroad, and vouchsafing to us in his mercy many and signal victories over the enemy, who is of our own household. It has also pleased our heavenly Father to favor as well our citizens in their homes as our soldiers in their camps and our sailors on the rivers and seas with unusual health. He has largely augmented our free population by emancipation and by immigration, while he has opened to us new sources of wealth, and has crowned the labor of our working men in every department of industry with abundant rewards. Moreover, he has been pleased to animate and inspire our minds and hearts with fortitude, courage and resolution sufficient for the great trial of civil war into which we have been brought by our adherence as a nation to the cause of freedom and humanity, and to afford to us reasonable hopes of an ultimate and happy deliverance from all our dangers and afflictions.

Now, therefore, I, Abraham Lincoln, President of the United States, do, hereby, appoint and set apart the last Thursday of November next as a day which I desire to be observed by all my fellow-citizens wherever they may then be as a day of thanksgiving and praise to Almighty God the beneficent Creator and Ruler of the universe. And I do farther recommend to my fellow-citizens aforesaid, that on that occasion they do reverently humble themselves in the dust and from thence offer up penitent and fervent prayers and supplications to the great Disposer of events for a return of the inestimable blessings of peace, union and harmony throughout the land which it has pleased him to assign as a dwelling place for ourselves and for our posterity throughout all generations.[21]

Mrs. Lydia Bixby was a Boston widow about whom Lincoln had been erroneously told that she had lost five sons (she had lost two) in the war. Although there is a debate among historians today as to whether or not the letter was written by Lincoln or one of his private secretaries,[22] it still serves as a model of tactful, heart-felt condolence.

To: Mrs. Lydia Bixby   Nov. 21, 1864

Dear Madam,

I have been shown in the files of the War Department a statement of the Adjutant General of Massachusetts, that you are the mother of five sons who have died gloriously on the field of battle.

I feel how weak and fruitless must be any words of mine which should attempt to beguile you from the grief of a loss so overwhelming. But I cannot refrain from tendering to you the consolation that may be found in the thanks of the Republic they died to save.

I pray that our Heavenly Father may assuage the anguish of your bereavement, and leave you only the cherished memory of the loved and lost, and the solemn pride that must be yours, to have laid so costly a sacrifice upon the altar of Freedom.[23]

The Second Inaugural Address is recognized as one of the world's great speeches. In it Lincoln eloquently expressed not only his own thoughts and conclusions about the meaning of the war, but also the anguish of his generation over the same. He concluded that God chose to use the war to punish the nation for slavery, and rather than allowing a speedy end to the conflict, chose to allow the war to go on for His own purposes.

The first part serves as an apology for the speech's brevity and as a summarization of the nation's war efforts to that time.

Second Inaugural Address, March 4, 1865,

Fellow Countrymen: At this second appearing to take the oath of the presidential office, there is less occasion for an extended address than there was at the first. Then a statement, somewhat in detail, of a course to be pursued, seemed fitting and proper. Now, at the expiration of four years, during which public declarations have been constantly called forth on every point and phase of the great contest which still absorbs the attention and engrosses the energies of the nation, little that is new could be presented. The progress of our arms, upon which all else chiefly depends, is as well known to the public as to myself; and it is, I trust, reasonably satisfactory and encouraging to all. With high hope for the future, no prediction in regard to it is ventured.

On the occasion corresponding to this four years ago, all thoughts were anxiously directed to an impending civil war. All dreaded it—all sought to avert it. While the inaugural address was being delivered from this place, devoted altogether to saving the Union without war, insurgent agents were in the city seeking to destroy it without war—seeking to dissolve the Union, and divide effects, by negotiation. Both parties deprecated war; but one of them would make war rather than let the nation survive; and the other would accept war rather than let it perish. And the war came.

Lincoln next attempted to explain the "cause" of the war. He acknowledged that slavery became the "powerful interest" and underlying basis.

One-eighth of the whole population were colored slaves, not distributed generally over the Union, but localized in the Southern part of it. These slaves constituted a peculiar and powerful interest. All knew that this interest was, somehow, the cause of the war. To strengthen, perpetuate, and extend this interest was the object for which the insurgents would rend the Union, even by war; while the government claimed no right to do more than to restrict the territorial enlargement of it.

Lincoln discussed his generation's surprise over the magnitude the war had attained, and exhorted the Northern people not to judge the Southern people for seeking God's blessing on their cause. He drew upon his knowledge of the Bible to support his conclusion that the Civil War was God's judgment upon the nation because of the offense of slavery.

Neither party expected for the war the magnitude or the duration which it has already attained. Neither anticipated that the cause of the conflict might cease with, or even before, the conflict itself should cease. Each looked for an easier triumph, and a result less fundamental and astounding. Both read the same Bible, and pray to the same God; and each invokes his aid against the other. It may seem strange that any men should dare to ask a just God's assistance in wringing their bread from the sweat of other men's faces; but let us judge not, that we be not judged. The prayers of both could not be answered—that of neither has been answered fully.

The Almighty has his own purposes. "Woe unto the world because of offenses! for it must needs be that offenses come; but woe to that man by whom the offense cometh." If we shall suppose that American slavery is one of those offenses which, in the providence of God, must needs come, but which, having continued through his appointed time, he now wills to remove, and that he gives to both North and South this terrible war, as the woe due to those by whom the offense came, shall we discern therein any departure from those divine attributes which the believers in a living God always ascribe to him? Fondly do we hope—fervently do we pray—that this mighty scourge of war may speedily pass away. Yet, if God wills that it continue until all the wealth piled by the bondman's two hundred and fifty years of unrequited toil shall be sunk, and until every drop of blood drawn with the lash shall be paid by another drawn with the sword, as was said three thousand years ago, so still it must be said, "The judgments of the Lord are true and righteous altogether."

His final words have become, to succeeding generations, among the most eloquent examples of Christian charity and statesmanship.

With malice toward none; with charity for all; with firmness in the right, as God gives us to see the right, let us strive on to finish the work we are in: to bind up the nation's wounds; to care for him who shall have borne the battle, and for his widow, and his orphan—to do all which may achieve and cherish a just and lasting peace among ourselves, and with all nations.[24]

Soon after the Second Inaugural Address, Lincoln received a letter from Thurlow Weed, Republican Party boss from New York, complimenting him on its message. In his response, Lincoln expressed belief he had heard God's voice on the issue of slavery, and confidence that history would judge his Second Inaugural to be one of his best speeches.

Letter to Thurlow Weed, March 15, 1865:

Every one likes a compliment. Thank you for yours on my little notification speech and on the recent inaugural address. I expect the latter to wear as well as—perhaps better than—anything I have produced; but I believe it is not immediately popular. Men are not flattered by being shown that there has been a difference of purpose between the Almighty and them. To deny it, however, in this case, is to deny that there is a God governing the world. It is a truth which I thought needed to be told, and, as whatever of humiliation there is in it falls most directly on myself, I thought others might afford for me to tell it.[25]

Chapter 9

Our Debt to Our Children

When Lincoln took office as president, many of the most influential men of his generation believed that he should allow the South to secede and form a separate nation. Lincoln could easily have done what the editor of the nation's most powerful newspaper suggested he do, let the Southern states "go in peace."[1] *But Lincoln saw more clearly than anyone the calamity that would befall not only his generation, but future generations, if he did so. He understood completely both his responsibility and debt to future generations, and the following speeches and writings illustrate this understanding.*

Lincoln revealed why he believed his generation must save the Union.

The struggle of today, is not altogether for today—it is for a vast future also.[2]

In May 1861, Lincoln explained to his secretary John Hay, who was later the secretary of state for William McKinley and Theodore Roosevelt, why he considered it essential that the Union be maintained.

For my part, I consider the central idea pervading this struggle is the necessity that is upon us, of proving that popular government is not an absurdity. We must settle this question now, whether in a free government the minority have the right to break up the government whenever they choose. If we fail it will go far to prove the incapability of the people to govern themselves.[3]

The following is illustrative of how Lincoln considered his most important mission to be that of preserving the Union and democratic government for future generations.

115

And this issue [civil war] embraces more than the fate of these United States. It presents to the whole family of man the question whether a constitutional republic or a democracy—a government of the people by the same people—can or cannot maintain its territorial integrity against its own domestic foes. It presents the question, whether discontented individuals, too few in numbers to control administration according to organic law, in any case, can always, upon the pretences made in this case, or on any other pretences, or arbitrarily without any pretence, break up their Government, and thus practically put an end to free government upon the earth. It forces us to ask: "Is there, in all republics, this inherent, and fatal weakness?" "Must a government, of necessity, be too strong for the liberties of its own people, or too weak to maintain its own existence?"[4]

In a speech Lincoln read to a crowd of well-wishers that came to greet him after he had won his second term as president, he demonstrated his pride in the fact that a democratic government could continue to function and hold national elections, even in the midst of a bitter Civil War.

It has long been a grave question whether any government, not too strong for the liberties of its people, can be strong enough to maintain its own existence, in great emergencies.

On this point the present rebellion brought our republic to a severe test; and a presidential election occurring in regular course during the rebellion added not a little to the strain. If the loyal people, united, were put to the utmost of their strength by the rebellion, must they not fail when divided, and partially paralyzed, by a political war among themselves?

But the election was a necessity.

We can not have free government without elections; and if the rebellion could force us to forego, or postpone a national election, it might fairly claim to have already conquered and ruined us. The strife of the election is but human-nature practically applied to the facts of the case. What has occurred in this case, must ever recur in similar cases. Human-nature will not change. In any future great national trial, compared with the men of this, we shall have as weak, and as strong; as silly and as wise; as bad and good. Let us, therefore, study the incidents of this, as philosophy to learn wisdom from, and none of them as wrongs to be revenged.

But the election, along with its incidental, and undesirable strife, has done good too. It has demonstrated that a people's government can sustain a national election, in the midst of a great civil war. Until now it has not been known to the world that this was a possibility. It shows also how sound, and how strong we still are. It shows that, even among candidates of the same party, he who is most devoted to the Union, and most opposed to treason, can receive most of the people's votes. It shows also, to the extent yet known, that we have more men now, than we had when the war began. Gold is good in its place; but living, brave, patriotic men, are better than gold.

But the rebellion continues; and now that the election is over, may not all, having a common interest, re-unite in a common effort, to save our common country? For my own part I have striven, and shall strive to avoid placing any obstacle in the way. So long as I have been here I have not willingly planted a thorn in any man's bosom.

While I am deeply sensible to the high compliment of a re-election; and duly grateful, as I trust, to Almighty God for having directed my countrymen to a right conclusion, as I think, for their own good, it adds nothing to my satisfaction that any other man may be disappointed or pained by the result.

May I ask those who have not differed with me, to join with me, in this same spirit towards those who have?

And now, let me close by asking three hearty cheers for our brave soldiers and seamen and their gallant and skilful commanders.[5]

When given an opportunity to talk to soldiers, Lincoln usually used the occasion to emphasize the importance of the war's outcome on future generations.

SOLDIERS—You are about to return to your homes and your friends, after having, as I learn, performed in camp a comparatively short term of duty in this great contest. I am greatly obliged to you, and to all who have come forward at the call of their country. I wish it might be more generally and universally understood what the country is now engaged in. We have, as all will agree, a free Government, where every man has a right to be equal with every other man. In this great struggle, this form of Government and every form of human right is endangered if our enemies succeed. There is more involved in this contest than is realized by every one. There is involved in this struggle the question whether your children and my children shall enjoy the privileges we have enjoyed. I say this in order to impress upon you, if you are not already so impressed, that no small matter should divert us from our great purpose. There may be some irregularities in the practical application of our system. It is fair that each man shall pay taxes in exact proportion to the value of his property; but if we should wait before collecting a tax to adjust the taxes upon each man in exact proportion with every other man, we should never collect any tax at all. There may be mistakes made sometimes; things may be done wrong while the officers of the Government do all they can to prevent mistakes. But I beg of you, as citizens of this great Republic, not to let your minds be carried off from the great work we have before us. This struggle is too large for you to be diverted from it by any small matter. When you return to your homes rise up to the height of a generation of men worthy of a free Government, and we will carry out the great work we have commenced. I return to you my sincere thanks, soldiers, for the honor you have done me this afternoon.[6]

Lincoln always encouraged soldiers by thanking them and expressing his belief that their sacrifices were as important to future generations as they were to their own.

I suppose you are going home to see your families and friends. For the service you have done in this great struggle in which we are engaged, I present you sincere thanks for myself and the country.

I almost always feel inclined, when I happen to say anything to soldiers, to impress upon them, in a few brief remarks, the importance of success in this contest. It is not merely for to-day, but for all time to come, that we should perpetuate for our children's children that great and free government, which we have enjoyed all our lives. I beg you to remember this, not merely for my sake, but for yours. I happen, temporarily, to occupy this White House. I am a living witness that any one of your children may look to come here as my father's child has. It is in order that each of you may have, through this free government which we have enjoyed, an open field and a fair chance for your industry, enterprise, and intelligence; that you may all have equal privileges in the race of life, with all its desirable human aspirations. It is for this the struggle should be maintained, that we may not lose our birthright—not only for one, but for two or three years. The nation is worth fighting for, to secure such an inestimable jewel.[7]

In the following Lincoln stated his belief the outcome of the war would impact the religious freedom as well as political freedom of future generations.

GENTLEMEN: I welcome here the representatives of the Evangelical Lutherans of the United States. I accept with gratitude their assurances of the sympathy and support of that enlightened, influential, and loyal class of my fellow-citizens in an important crisis which involves, in my judgment, not only the civil and religious liberties of our own dear land, but in a large degree the civil and religious liberties of mankind in many countries and through many ages. You well know, gentlemen, and the world knows, how reluctantly I accepted this issue of battle forced upon me, on my advent to this place, by the internal enemies of our country. You all know, the world knows the forces and resources the public agents have brought into employment to sustain a Government against which there has been brought not one complaint of real injury committed against society, at home or abroad. You all may recollect that in taking up the sword thus forced into our hands this Government appealed to the prayers of the pious and the good, and declared that it placed its whole dependence upon the favor of God. I now humbly and reverently, in your presence, reiterate the acknowledgment of that dependence, not doubting that, if it shall please the Divine Being who determines the destinies of nations that this shall remain a united people, they will, humbly seeking the Divine guidance, make their prolonged national existence a source of new benefits to themselves and their successors, and to all classes and conditions of mankind.[8]

As he always did when talking to soldiers, Lincoln attempted to communicate his sense of the importance of their efforts to save the Union, and, consequently, democratic government.

SOLDIERS of the 148th Ohio:—I am most happy to meet you on this occasion. I understand that it has been your honorable privilege to stand, for a brief period, in the defense of your country, and that now you are on your way to your homes. I congratulate you, and those who are waiting to bid you welcome home from the war; and permit me, in the name of the people, to thank you for the part you have taken in this struggle for the life of the nation. You are soldiers of the republic, everywhere honored and respected. Whenever I appear before a body of soldiers, I feel tempted to talk to them of the nature of the struggle in which we are engaged. I look upon it as an attempt on the one hand to overwhelm and destroy the national existence, while, on our part, we are striving to maintain the government and institutions of our fathers, to enjoy them ourselves, and transmit them to our children and our children's children forever.

To do this the constitutional administration of our government must be sustained, and I beg of you not to allow your minds or your hearts to be diverted from the support of all necessary measures for that purpose, by any miserable picayune arguments addressed to your pockets, or inflammatory appeals made to your passions or your prejudices.

It is vain and foolish to arraign this man or that for the part he has taken, or has not taken, and to hold the government responsible for his acts. In no administration can there be perfect equality of action and uniform satisfaction rendered by all.

But this government must be preserved in spite of the acts of any man or set of men. It is worthy your every effort. Nowhere in the world is presented a government of so much liberty and equality. To the humblest and poorest amongst us are held out the highest privileges and positions. The present moment finds me at the White House, yet there is as good a chance for your children as there was for my father's.

Again I admonish you not to be turned from your stern purpose of defending your beloved country and its free institutions by any arguments urged by ambitious and designing men, but stand fast to the Union and the old flag. Soldiers, I bid you God-speed to your homes.[9]

---

*In this excerpt from the end of his annual messages to Congress in 1864, Lincoln
expressed his satisfaction that the elections proved the people were committed to
maintaining the Union.*

The most reliable indication of public purpose in this country is derived through our popular elections. Judging by the recent canvass and its
result, the purpose of the people within the loyal States to maintain the
integrity of the Union, was never more firm nor more nearly unanimous
than now. The extraordinary calmness and good order with which the millions of voters met and mingled at the polls give strong assurance of this.
Not only all those who supported the Union ticket, so called, but a great
majority of the opposing party also, may be fairly claimed to entertain, and
to be actuated by, the same purpose. It is an unanswerable argument to
this effect, that no candidate for any office whatever, high or low, has ventured to seek votes on the avowal that he was for giving up the Union.
There have been much impugning of motives, and much heated controversy as to the proper means and best mode of advancing the Union cause;
but on the distinct issue of Union or no Union, the politicians have shown
their instinctive knowledge that there is no diversity among the people. In
affording the people the fair opportunity of showing one to another and to
the world this firmness and unanimity of purpose, the election has been of
vast value to the national cause.[10]

Afterword

Lincoln believed that while he was president he must "work out [God's] great purposes." Pursuant to this, he had "sought His aid" so that his "works and acts [would] be according to His will."[1] Lincoln became convinced that it would have been against the will of God and the intention of the nation's founders to allow the Union to dissolve and a Southern nation form upon the basis of slavery. Consequently, he resolved to do everything within his power, including a liberal interpretation of the war powers assigned him as commander in chief, to save the Union and preserve the proposition that "all men are created equal."

Lincoln once said that if he were remembered by history it would be for freeing the slaves, but contemporary critics have attempted to belittle his efforts in this. The most vocal of his detractors criticize the Emancipation Proclamation, and sagely proclaim that the document "freed no slaves."[2] This criticism is of dubious value, but even if it were not, it should be remembered that Lincoln did not stop with the Emancipation Proclamation in his fight against slavery. Recognizing the Emancipation Proclamation was useful only as a war measure, he put significant effort into passing the constitutional amendment that legally abolished slavery. Four months after the Emancipation Proclamation had taken effect, when Congress failed to muster the necessary two-thirds majority to pass the amendment, Lincoln intervened. He used all of his political skill to secure the necessary votes, and the House of Representatives approved the Thirteenth Amendment on January 31, 1864.[3] Congress then sent it to the states for their ratification.

The Thirteenth Amendment was not ratified by the required majority of 27 states until December 18, 1865. By this time, slavery had been virtually nonexistent for more than six months. In spite of all the modern-day criticism, the Emancipation Proclamation has proven itself to have been a very useful document.

121

Today's critics of Lincoln have also attacked his "motive" for abolishing slavery. A few have claimed he was really a White Supremacist that had no true concern for African-Americans, and his reason for eliminating slavery was simply to benefit the white race.[4] They have attempted to justify this claim by taking some of Lincoln's statements out of context and ignoring the overwhelming evidence that he did, in fact, want to help the black race.[5] In 1876, a more sympathetic Frederick Douglass attempted to explain Lincoln's complicated task:

"I have said that President Lincoln was a white man, and shared the prejudices common to his countrymen towards the colored race. Looking back to his times and to the condition of his country, we are compelled to admit that this unfriendly feeling on his part may be safely set down as one element of his wonderful success in organizing the American people for the tremendous conflict before them safely through the conflict.

His great mission was to accomplish two things: first, to save his country from dismemberment and ruin; and second, to free his country from the great crime of slavery. To do one or the other, or both, he must have the earnest sympathy and the powerful co-operation of his loyal fellow-countrymen. Without this primary and essential condition to success his efforts must have been vain and utterly fruitless. Had he put the abolition of slavery before the salvation of the Union, he would have inevitably driven from him a powerful class of the American people and rendered resistance to rebellion impossible. Viewed from the genuine abolition ground, Mr. Lincoln seemed tardy, cold, dull, and indifferent; but measuring him by the sentiment of his country, a sentiment he was bound as a statesman to consult, he was swift, zealous, radical, and determined."[6]

As far as the charge of Lincoln's "prejudice" towards the black race, one must consider not only Douglass' statement above, but also what he said about Lincoln during the Civil War: "I was impressed with his [Lincoln's] entire freedom from popular prejudice against the colored race. He was the first great man that I talked with in the United States freely, who in no single instance reminded me of the difference between himself and myself, of the difference of color . . . I felt as though I was in the presence of a big brother, and that there was safety in his atmosphere."[7]

Douglass, who knew Lincoln better than any other African-American, seemed somewhat confused about the sixteenth president's relationship with the black race. But he was not as confused as William Herndon and others were about Lincoln's relationship with God. In their attempts to explain Lincoln's religious beliefs, many people have fallen into the trap of trying to classify him as agnostic, deist, Christian, or any number of other things. Taking into account his speeches and writings, Lincoln does not fit conveniently, or at least completely, into any of these groups.

Early biographers of Lincoln stated he was a Christian, but Herndon disagreed. He argued against this claim for many years, but eventually came to realize how little he really knew about Lincoln's religious beliefs. Seventeen years after Lincoln's death, Herndon wrote, "I do not say he was a Christian. I do not say that he was not. I give no opinion the one way or the other. I simply state facts and let each person judge for himself."[8] Nevertheless, Herndon believed the Almighty used Lincoln and said: "God rolled Mr. Lincoln through his fiery furnace specially—that he might be His instrument in the future. This purifying process gave Mr. Lincoln charity, liberality, kindness, tenderness, toleration, a sublime faith . . . in the purposes and ends of his Maker."[9]

When reminiscing about Lincoln, William Herndon once stated, "I cannot say I comprehended him."[10] Hundreds of persons, including his friends, biographers, historians, and psychologists have tried

Lincoln's law partner William Herndon, who interviewed hundreds of people that knew Lincoln and wrote a comprehensive biography about him.
Courtesy of the Illinois State Historical Library

to understand Lincoln's personality and opinions on subjects such as his relationship with the black race, women, and God. He had a streak of melancholy in his nature, and this is commonly perceived as one of the reasons he is so difficult to figure out. He was very reluctant to talk about his inner feelings, and outwardly seemed to be a combination of disparate parts. On one side there was the crude, jocular Lincoln that loved jokes and homely stories. On the other was the pensive intellectual that memorized Scripture, poetry, and Shakespeare. Another side of Lincoln was the wily politician and stump speaker, whose opposite was the eloquent spokesman for freedom and democracy. Finally, there was the confident president that curtly hired and fired major generals on the eve of significant battles, balanced by the unassuming leader that quietly admitted, "I claim not to have controlled events, but confess plainly that events have controlled me."[11]

Unfortunately, Lincoln did not have the opportunity to finish the work begun with the Emancipation Proclamation and the Thirteenth Amendment. If he had, America might face significantly less racial strife today. But he understood how his personal life served as an example for others—regardless of their race. Booker T. Washington, in assessing Lincoln's life, once said of him: "In his rise from the most abject poverty and ignorance to a position of high usefulness and power, he taught the world one of the greatest of all lessons. In fighting his own battle up from obscurity and squalor, he fought the battle of every other individual and race that is down, and so helped to pull up every other human who was down."[12]

Although he did not live to see the proposition of equality expressed in the Declaration of Independence fully realized, Lincoln at least had the satisfaction of knowing he had accomplished the great task that faced him when he became president—the successful prosecution of the war and the preservation of the Union. In preserving government "of the people, by the people, and for the people," he believed that the nation had a chance for "a new birth of freedom."[13] In accomplishing these tasks, Lincoln proved that he was truly God's man for the hour—"a humble instrument in the hands of our Heavenly Father."[14]

Acknowledgments

First and foremost, I am greatly indebted to my friend Clark Evans, senior reference librarian of the Rare Book and Special Collections Reading Room at the Library of Congress, for his invaluable assistance. Clark is the president of the Abraham Lincoln Institute of the Mid-Atlantic, and his knowledge of Lincoln and research skills are something that I've been fortunate enough to experience firsthand, especially when I needed help in verifying authenticity and tracking down sources for Lincoln quotes.

Many thanks are due Ed Bearss, historian emeritus of the National Park Service, and historian Ed Steers for carefully reading the manuscript and providing countless corrections and suggested improvements. Also, special thanks to Michael Burlingame of Connecticut College for his willingness to take time out of his busy schedule to review the manuscript, provide corrections, and prepare an introduction for this book. Any remaining errors or misinterpretations in the book are due to my own oversight, and not theirs.

Thanks to historians Douglas Wilson and Rodney Davis, of the Lincoln Studies Center at Knox College, for their efforts to locate some Herndon material for me. Also, I would here like to voice my appreciation of their book *Herndon's Informants*, whose publication was probably one of the three or four most significant accomplishments in the world of Lincoln historiography in the 20th century.

My thanks to Harold Collier and Martin Gordon of White Mane Publishing Company for sharing my vision for *Lincoln on God and Country* and providing invaluable guidance on the manuscript. Also, many thanks are due to the talented staff of White Mane Publishers and Beidel Printing House for their patience and expertise.

During the course of working on the book, I have received encouragement and assistance from many friends and family members. First among these has been my father-in-law, Buddy Norris of Bryantown, Maryland. He has always encouraged me to "stick with it" and in doing so deserves some of the credit for its completion. Also I would like to thank my friends at the Lincoln Group of the District of Columbia, and Abraham Lincoln Institute of the Mid-Atlantic for their enthusiasm and interest.

I would like to thank my wife and children for putting up with my work on this book for so long. I've tried to limit the bulk of the time spent on it to the late evening hours, when Jean's homeschooling work was finished and our family time was over, but this became increasingly difficult to do over the last few months. Thanks are also due to Jean for helping with the proofreading and providing invaluable suggestions for improvements to the manuscript. Again, my thanks to Daniel, Jason, and Michael for putting up with Dad's mental absence.

Finally, I close with Psalm 107:1—Give thanks to the Lord, for He is good.

Notes

Preface

1. Nicolay and Hay, editors, *Complete Works of Lincoln*, (hereafter Nicolay), vol. 2, 227–28.
2. William H. Herndon, *Herndon's Life of Lincoln*, 360.
3. Ibid., 359.
4. Ibid., 360.
5. In a letter recorded in Emanuel Hertz's *The Hidden Lincoln*, p. 91, Herndon writes, "I said to you in a private letter that Mr. Lincoln was at all times and places and under all circumstances a deeply and a thoroughly religious man, sincerely, firmly, broadly, and grandly so. I do not say he was a Christian. I do not say that he was not. I give no opinion the one way or the other. I simply state facts and let each person judge for himself." This letter was dated November 24, 1882. My thanks to Michael Burlingame of Connecticut College and Douglas L. Wilson and Rodney O. Davis of Knox College in their efforts to try to locate the original of this document.

Introduction

1. Benjamin P. Thomas, "The Individuality of Lincoln," *Bulletin of the Abraham Lincoln Association*, no. 32 (September 1933), 3.
2. Wilson and Davis, eds., *Herndon's Informants*, 202–3. Robert L. Wilson to Herndon, Sterling, Illinois, 10 February 1866.
3. On Hill's opposition to Lincoln, see Jay Monaghan, "New Light on the Lincoln-Rutledge Romance," *Abraham Lincoln Quarterly* 3 (1944): 138–45.
4. John Hill to Ida M. Tarbell, Columbus, Georgia, 4 April 1896, Tarbell Papers, Allegheny College.
5. John Hill to Ida M. Tarbell, Columbus, Georgia, 17 February 1896, copy, Tarbell Papers, Allegheny College.
6. Albert Taylor Bledsoe, review of Ward Hill Lamon's biography of Lincoln, *The Southern Review*, 12 (April 1873): 333–34.
7. Ibid., 360–61.
8. See Michael Burlingame, *The Inner World of Abraham Lincoln*, 1–19.
9. Benjamin P. Thomas, *Abraham Lincoln: A Biography*, 130, 143.
10. Albert J. Beveridge, *Abraham Lincoln, 1809–1858*, 2 vols., 1: 493, 2: 244.
11. Count S. Stakelberg, "Tolstoi Holds Lincoln World's Greatest Hero," *New York World*, 7 February 1901.

Chapter 1—Lincoln's Life

1. From Lamon, *Life of Abraham Lincoln*, 39–40; and Carl Sandburg, *The Prairie Years*, vol. 1, 61.
2. Now Larue County.
3. Wilson and Davis, *Herndon's Informants*, 726, Dennis Hanks testimony.
4. Matthew 22:37 and 39; Don E. Fehrenbacher and Virginia Fehrenbacher, *Recollected Words*, 137.
5. Now Spencer County.
6. Louis Warren, *Lincoln's Youth*, 20.
7. Ibid., 28–29.
8. Wilson and Davis, *Herndon's Informants*, 40, Dennis Hanks testimony.
9. William J. Wolf, *The Religion of Abraham Lincoln*, 35.
10. David Donald, *Lincoln*, 36.
11. Beveridge, *Abraham Lincoln*, vol. 1, 125.
12. Wilson and Davis, *Herndon's Informants*, 386, Robert Rutledge testimony.
13. Roy P. Basler, *Collected Works of Abraham Lincoln*, (hereafter Basler), vol. 1, 7.
14. Elton Trueblood, *Abraham Lincoln: Theologian of American Anguish*, 16; see also Allen Guelzo's *Abraham Lincoln: Redeemer President*, chapter 3, for a more thorough explanation of the "Doctrine of Necessity."
15. US Senator Paul Simon, who wrote the definitive study on Lincoln's years in the state legislature, researched the voting records of both supporters and opponents of the Springfield move and compared them to the voting records of recipients of Internal Improvements. He concludes that "there is no evidence that Lincoln supported any measure with which he was in basic disagreement in order to secure votes for Springfield." See Simon's *Lincoln's Preparation for Greatness: The Illinois Legislative Years*, 104.
16. See Douglas Wilson's *Honor Voice: The Transformation of Abraham Lincoln*, chapter 7 for detailed dicussion about Lincoln and Mary Todd.
17. Simon, *Lincoln's Preparation for Greatness*, 214.
18. Nicolay, vol. 1, 218–19.
19. Stephen Oates, *With Malice Toward None*, 45.
20. John J. Duff, *Abraham Lincoln: Prairie Lawyer*, 170.
21. Ibid., 86–87.
22. Edgar DeWitt Jones, *Lincoln and the Preachers*, 44.
23. Nicolay, vol. 8, 33.
24. Thomas, *Abraham Lincoln*, 182.
25. Nicolay, vol. 5, 127.
26. Lincoln's secretary of war, Edwin Stanton, imprisoned thousands of people during the war. But those incarcerated were genuinely believed to be a threat to the North's war effort, and were rarely jailed, as historian Mark Neely points out, for "anything to do with conventional politics." This matter was handled in an equitable manner, and Congress had no difficulty endorsing Lincoln's temporary suspensions of habeas corpus. See Mark Neely's *The Fate of Liberty*, p. 233 and Ed Steers' *His Name is Still Mudd*, p. 92, for elaboration.
27. Nicolay, vol. 6, 342.
28. Emanuel Hertz, *Lincoln Talks*, 459.
29. Bruce Catton, *Grant Moves South*, 371.
30. Oates, *With Malice Toward None*, 293.
31. Allen T. Rice, *Reminiscences of Abraham Lincoln*, 193–95.
32. Nicolay, vol. 3, 33.

33. In the course of changing the war's purpose Lincoln demonstrated what modern leadership theorists would recognize as both transformational and transactional leadership skills. See Gordon Leidner's "Measuring the Presidents: Modern leadership theory provides a framework for comparing the presidential skills of Lincoln and Davis" in *Columbiad: A Quarterly Review of the War Between the States,* vol. 2, no. 1, 61–76.

34. Nicolay, vol. 8, 67.

35. Mark Neely, *Abraham Lincoln Encyclopedia,* 151.

36. For further discussion, see Gary Wills, *Lincoln at Gettysburg,* chapter 4: "Revolution in Thought."

37. See Davis, *Lincoln's Men,* chapter 7, for more detail. Also, my thanks to Ed Steers for pointing out that Lincoln mandated all capital cases be sent to him for review.

38. Oates, *With Malice Toward None,* 224.

39. Joshua Speed, *Reminiscences of Abraham Lincoln and Notes of a Visit to California,* 32–33; also Fehrenbacher, *Recollected Words,* 414.

40. Nicolay, vol. 10, 215–16.

41. Miers, *Lincoln Day by Day,* vol. 3, p. 325.

42. Carpenter, *Six Months in the White House,* 209.

43. Bishop, *The Day Lincoln Was Shot,* 295.

Chapter 2—Our Debt to the Nation's Founders

1. Nicolay, vol. 1, 48.
2. Nicolay, vol. 2, 228–30.
3. Basler, vol. 2, 406.
4. Basler, vol. 2, 499–501.
5. Basler, vol. 2, 545–47.
6. Nicolay, vol. 5, 59–65.
7. Nicolay, vol. 6, 157.
8. Basler, vol. 4, 168–69.

Chapter 3—The People

1. Nicolay, vol. 1, 26.
2. Nicolay, vol. 1, 35–43.
3. Nicolay, vol. 5, 232.
4. Basler, vol. 4, 144.
5. Nicolay, vol. 6, 121.
6. Nicolay, vol. 6, 183.
7. Nicolay, vol. 6, 141–42.
8. Basler, vol. 4, 228.
9. Nicolay, vol. 6, 160–61.
10. Nicolay, vol. 6, 183.
11. Nicolay, vol. 6, 312.
12. Nicolay, vol. 6, 321.
13. Basler, vol. 4, 88.

Chapter 4—Government and Economy

1. Nicolay, vol. 3, 252.
2. Basler, vol. 1, 148.
3. Nicolay, vol. 1, 137–39.

4. Basler, vol. 1, 438.
5. Nicolay, vol. 2, 37.
6. Nicolay, vol. 2, 144–46.
7. Nicolay, vol. 2, 186–87.
8. Nicolay, vol. 2, 184.
9. Basler, vol. 3, 453.
10. Nicolay, vol. 2, 310.
11. Basler, vol. 2, 532.
12. Basler, vol. 3, 478–79.
13. Nicolay, vol. 5, 360–61.
14. Nicolay, vol. 6, 150–51.
15. Nicolay, vol. 6, 173–75.
16. Basler, vol. 5, 43.
17. Nicolay, vol. 8, 288.

Chapter 5—Law and Politics

1. Nicolay, vol. 1, 1–9.
2. Nicolay, vol. 1, 14–15.
3. Nicolay, vol. 1, 15–16.
4. Nicolay, vol. 1, 27.
5. Nicolay, vol. 2, 49–50.
6. Nicolay, vol. 2, 140–43.
7. Nicolay, vol. 2, 75–76.
8. Nicolay, vol. 2, 88.
9. Basler, vol. 2, 126.
10. Nicolay, vol. 2, 333–34.
11. Basler, vol. 2, 469.
12. Basler, vol. 2, 506.
13. Nicolay, vol. 4, 379–80.
14. Zall, P. M. ed., *Abe Lincoln Laughing*, 5.
15. Nicolay, vol. 5, 125.
16. Basler, vol. 4, 121.
17. Nicolay, vol. 6, 72.
18. Nicolay, vol. 8, 157.

Chapter 6—Freedom

1. Basler, vol. 1, 74–75.
2. Basler, vol. 2, 115.
3. Nicolay, vol. 2, 184.
4. Nicolay, vol. 2, 205–48.
5. Basler, vol. 2, 318.
6. The Know-Nothing party shunned Catholics, Jews, and immigrants.
7. Nicolay, vol. 2, 287.
8. Nicolay, vol. 2, 338.
9. Nicolay, vol. 2, 329–30.
10. Nicolay, vol. 3, 1–2.

11. Nicolay, vol. 3, 49–51.
12. Basler, vol. 2, 520–21.
13. Basler, vol. 3, 16.
14. Basler, vol. 3, 181.
15. Nicolay, vol 4, 262–63
16. In the 1850s, U.S. Senators were chosen by the state legislatures, instead of the direct vote of the people, as today.
17. Nicolay, vol. 5, 94.
18. Nicolay, vol. 5, 95.
19. Nicolay, vol. 5, 126.
20. Basler, vol. 3, 436.
21. Basler, vol. 3, 440–41, 453–54.
22. Basler, vol. 4, 149–50.
23. Basler, vol. 4, 183.
24. Basler, vol. 2, 353.
25. Basler, vol. 2, 95–96.
26. Basler, vol. 2, 281.
27. Nicolay, vol. 5, 326–28.
28. Nicolay, vol. 6, 8.
29. Basler, vol. 8, 360.
30. Nicolay, vol. 10, 77.
31. Nicolay, vol. 6, 110–11.

Chapter 7—Presidential Leadership

1. Nicolay, vol. 1, 138.
2. Nicolay, vol. 6, 184.
3. Nicolay, vol. 6, 322–25.
4. Pratt, *Concerning Mr. Lincoln*, 52; see also Fehrenbacher, *Recollected Words*, 254.
5. Burlingame, *The Inner World of Abraham Lincoln*, 183.
6. Basler, vol. 5, 185.
7. Nicolay, vol. 7, 240.
8. Nicolay, vol. 7, 298.
9. Nicolay, vol. 8, 15–16.
10. Nicolay, vol. 8, 37.
11. See David Long, *"Wartime Democracy: Lincoln and the Midterm Election of 1862,"* 110, for analysis.
12. Nicolay, vol. 8, 84–85.
13. Nicolay, vol. 8, 131.
14. Nicolay, vol. 8, 206–7.
15. Schuyler Colfax, *Life and Principles of Abraham Lincoln*, 18.
16. Nicolay, vol. 8, 308.
17. Nicolay, vol. 9, 26.
18. Basler, vol. 6, 410.
19. Nicolay, vol. 11, 209–10.
20. Basler, vol. 7, 253.
21. Nicolay, vol. 10, 65–66.

22. Carpenter, *Six Months in the White House*, 76–77.

23. Nicolay, vol. 10, 307–10.

24. Basler, vol. 8, 52.

25. Basler, vol. 8, 96.

Chapter 8—Faith in God

1. Trueblood, *Abraham Lincoln: Theologian of American Anguish*, 110; and Fehrenbacher, *Recollected Words*, 137.

2. Basler, vol. 1, 382.

3. Basler, vol. 2, 501.

4. Basler, vol. 3, 204.

5. Basler, vol. 5, 356.

6. Nicolay, vol. 6, 184.

7. Nicolay, vol. 6, 341–43.

8. Michael Burlingame, *Oral History of Abraham Lincoln*, 54.

9. Nicolay, vol. 7, 293.

10. Nicolay, vol. 8, 52–53.

11. Nicolay, vol. 8, 50–51.

12. Nicolay, vol. 8, 174.

13. Nicolay, vol. 8, 235–36.

14. Nicolay, vol. 9, 32–33.

15. In 1939, Franklin Roosevelt decided to move Thanksgiving up one week in order to provide a longer Christmas shopping season. Subsequently, however, it has been moved back to Lincoln's original date.

16. Nicolay, vol. 9, 151–53.

17. Basler, vol. 6, 536.

18. Nicolay, vol. 10, 149.

19. Nicolay, vol. 10, 215–16.

20. Basler, vol. 7, 542.

21. Nicolay, vol. 10, 245–46.

22. See Burlingame, "The Trouble with Lincoln's Bixby Letter," *American Heritage*, August 1999, 64–67.

23. Basler, vol. 8, 116–17.

24. Nicolay, vol. 11, 44–47.

25. Nicolay, vol. 11, 54.

Chapter 9—Our Debt to Our Children

1. David Donald, *Lincoln*, 287.

2. Nicolay, vol. 7, 60.

3. Tyler Dennett, *Lincoln and the Civil War In the Diaries and Letters of John Hay*, 19–20.

4. Nicolay, vol. 6, 304.

5. Basler, vol. 8, 101.

6. Basler, vol. 6, 505.

7. Nicolay, vol. 10, 202–3.

8. Basler, vol. 5, 212.

9. Nicolay, vol. 10, 208–9.

10. Nicolay, vol. 10, 304–5.

Afterword

1. Nicolay, vol. 8, 50–51.

2. For typical criticisms of the Emancipation Proclamation's effectiveness, see Lerome Bennett, "Was Abe Lincoln a White Supremacist?" *Ebony*, 40 (Feb. 1968, 37) and Barbara J. Fields "Who Freed the Slaves?" in Geoffrey C. Ward's *The Civil War: An Illustrated History*, New York: Alfred A. Knopf, 1991, 178–81.

3. David Long, *Jewel of Liberty*, 264.

4. Bennett, 23.

5. See Fehrenbacher, "Only His Stepchildren" from *Lincoln in Text and Context: Collected Essays* by Don E. Fehrenbacher, Stanford, Calif.: Stanford University Press, 1987, 95–112 for rebuttal of the racism claims and a balanced assessment of Lincoln's relationship with African Americans. See also McPherson, "Who Freed the Slaves?" from *Drawn With the Sword* by James McPherson, Oxford University Press, 1996, 192–207 for rebuttal of the argument that Lincoln deserves no credit for freeing the slaves.

6. Waldo Braden, *Building the Myth: Selected Speeches Memorializing Abraham Lincoln*, 98–99.

7. Rice, *Reminiscences of Abraham Lincoln*, 193–95.

8. Hertz, *The Hidden Lincoln*, 91.

9. Ibid., 43.

10. David Donald, *Lincoln's Herndon*, New York: Alfred A. Knopf, 1948, 305.

11. Basler, vol. 7, 282.

12. Braden, 155.

13. Nicolay, vol. 9, 210.

14. Nicolay, vol. 8, 50.

Sources

To assemble even a short book of Lincoln quotations with limited biographical information and editorial comment it was necessary to consult dozens of books and articles. Rather than attempting to cite everything, in the interest of saving space I have listed only primary sources. I regret that I cannot provide a more complete list of the Lincoln material I found helpful.

My basic sources for Lincoln's writings are *The Collected Works of Abraham Lincoln*, 8 vols., Roy P. Basler, ed., Marion Dolores Pratt and Lloyd A. Dunlap, asst. eds., published in 1955 by the Rutgers University Press and *The Complete Works of Abraham Lincoln*, John G. Nicolay, and John Hay, eds., published by Francis D. Tandy in 1905. Basler's work is the most recent and now available electronically from the Abraham Lincoln Association of Springfield, Illinois. Nicolay and Hay were Lincoln's secretaries and assembled the earliest comprehensive collection of Lincoln's writings. In the interest of referring to the earliest source, I have referenced Nicolay and Hay more frequently than Basler, but both are considered generally reliable by scholars.

In addition to the general works above, *Lincoln Day by Day: A Chronology, 1809–1865* by Earl S. Miers is an invaluable source for a chronology of Lincoln's life; Don E. and Virginia Fehrenbacher's *Recollected Words of Abraham Lincoln* is priceless for determining the reliability of Lincoln quotes not in Basler or Nicolay; Douglas Wilson and Rodney Davis' *Herndon's Informants: Letters, Interviews, and Statements About Abraham Lincoln* is the superbly edited collection of the William Herndon papers; and Mark Neely's *The Abraham Lincoln Encyclopedia* is an excellent, succinct guide to just about everything Lincoln, from his opinion about the Declaration of Independence and the Constitution to his impact on American history.

I have tried to confine my footnotes to sources for the quotations and a limited elaboration on facts. I have done my best to quote my sources accurately. I do not try to correct Lincoln's punctuation or spelling, or point out his errors with [*sic*], except in cases when I believe it essential for clarity.

Primary Sources for the Biography: General Works

Primary sources that have been influential in my understanding of Lincoln include Albert Beveridge's *Abraham Lincoln: 1809–1858*; Michael Burlingame's *The Inner World of Abraham Lincoln*; David Donald's *Lincoln*; William Herndon's *Herndon's Life of Lincoln*; James McPherson's *Battle Cry of Freedom*; Mark Neely's *The Last Best Hope of Earth*; Stephen Oates' *With Malice Toward None*; and Benjamin Thomas' *Abraham Lincoln*.

Primary sources for Lincoln's religious beliefs are Allen C. Guelzo's *Abraham Lincoln: Redeemer President*; David Hein's "The Calvinistic Tenor of Abraham Lincoln's Religious Thought" in *The Lincoln Herald*, vol. 85, no. 4; Wayne C. Temple's *Abraham Lincoln: From Skeptic to Prophet*; Elton Trueblood's *Abraham Lincoln, Theologian of American Anguish*; and William Wolf's *The Religion of Abraham Lincoln*. Dr. Guelzo's book is the newest and by far most comprehensive work on Lincoln's religious beliefs.

Primary Sources for the Biography: Specialized

In addition to the general works listed above, I found the following to be useful in preparation of these specific parts of the biography:

Youth

Primary sources are William Herndon's *Herndon's Life of Lincoln*, and Louis A. Warren's *Lincoln's Youth: Indiana Years*.

Young Legislator

Primary sources are Gabor S. Boritt's *Lincoln and the Economics of the American Dream*; Paul Simon's *Lincoln's Preparation for Greatness: The Illinois Legislative Years*; and Benjamin Thomas' *Lincoln's New Salem*.

Midlife

Primary sources are John Duff's *A. Lincoln: Prairie Lawyer*; John Frank's *Lincoln as a Lawyer*; Donald Wayne Riddle's *Lincoln Runs for Congress*; and Douglas L. Wilson's *Honor's Voice*.

The Spokesman

Primary sources are Don E. Fehrenbacher's *Prelude to Greatness* and William Baringer's *Lincoln's Rise to Power*, Harold Holzer's *The Lincoln-Douglas Debates*, Harry Jaffa's *Crisis of the House Divided*, and Allan Nevins' *The Emergence of Lincoln*.

The Leader and The Statesman

Primary sources are Ed Bearss' *The Campaign for Vicksburg: Grant Strikes a Fatal Blow*; Gabor Boritt's *Lincoln the War President: The Gettysburg Lectures*;

F. B. Carpenter's *Inner Life of Abraham Lincoln*; Bruce Catton's *The Coming Fury*, and *Grant Moves South*; Richard Current's *Speaking of Abraham Lincoln*; Eric Foner's *Reconstruction*; William E. Gienapp's "Abraham Lincoln and Presidential Leadership" in *We Cannot Escape History: Lincoln and the Last Best Hope of Earth*, James McPherson, ed.; Herman Hattaway's *How the North Won*; Burton Hendrick's *Lincoln's War Cabinet*; David Long's *The Jewel of Liberty*; Mark Neely's *The Fate of Liberty*; Phillip Shaw Paludan's *The Presidency of Abraham Lincoln*; Merrill D. Peterson's *Lincoln in American Memory*; J. G. Randall's *Lincoln the President: Springfield to Gettysburg*, and *Midstream*; Carl Sandburg's *Abraham Lincoln: The War Years*; Charles B. Strozier's *Lincoln's Quest for Union: Public and Private Meanings*; and Thomas Williams' *Lincoln and the Generals*.

Bibliography

Baringer, William. *Lincoln's Rise to Power*. Boston: Little, Brown, and Company, 1937.

Basler, Roy P., ed., Marion Dolores Pratt and Lloyd A. Dunlap, asst. eds., *The Collected Works of Abraham Lincoln*. New Brunswick, N.J.: Rutgers University Press, 1955.

Bearss, Edwin C. *The Campaign for Vicksburg: Grant Strikes a Fatal Blow*. Dayton, Ohio: Morningside, 1995.

Bennett, Lerome. "Was Abe Lincoln a white supremacist?" *Ebony*, 40 (February 1968).

Beveridge, Albert J. *Abraham Lincoln 1809–1858*, 2 vols. New York: Houghton Mifflin Company, 1928.

Bishop, Jim. *The Day Lincoln Was Shot*. New York: Harper and Brothers, 1955.

Bledsoe, Albert Taylor. "Review of Ward Hill Lamon's biography of Lincoln," *The Southern Review*, 12 (April 1873).

Boritt, Gabor S. *Lincoln and the Economics of the American Dream*. Urbana, Ill.: University of Illinois Press, 1994.

Boritt, Gabor S. *Lincoln the War President: The Gettysburg Lectures*. New York: Oxford University Press, 1992.

Braden, Waldo, ed. *Building the Myth: Selected Speeches Memorializing Abraham Lincoln*. Urbana, Ill.: University of Illinois Press, 1990.

Burlingame, Michael. *The Inner World of Abraham Lincoln*, Urbana, Ill.: University of Illinois Press, 1994.

———. *An Oral History of Abraham Lincoln: John G. Nicolay's Interviews and Essays*. Carbondale: Southern Illinois University Press, 1996.

Carpenter, F. B. *The Inner Life of Abraham Lincoln*. Boston: Houghton Mifflin & Co., 1883.

Catton, Bruce. *The Coming Fury*. New York: Doubleday, 1961.

———. *Grant Moves South*. Boston: Little, Brown, and Company, 1960.

Colfax, Schuyler. *Life and Principles of Abraham Lincoln*. Philadelphia: James B. Rodgers, 1865.

Current, Richard Nelson. *Speaking of Abraham Lincoln: The Man and His Meaning for Our Times* Urbana, Ill.: University of Illinois Press, 1983.

Davis, William C. *Lincoln's Men: How President Lincoln Became a Father to an Army and a Nation*. New York: Free Press, 1999.

Dennett, Tyler. *Lincoln and the Civil War In the Diaries and Letters of John Hay*. New York: Dodd, Mead, and Company, 1939.

Donald, David H. *Lincoln's Herndon*. New York: Alfred A. Knopf, 1948.

———. *Lincoln*. New York: Touchstone, 1996.

Duff, John J. *Abraham Lincoln, Prairie Lawyer*. New York: Rinehart and Company, 1960.

Fehrenbacher, Don E. *Prelude to Greatness: Lincoln in the 1850s*. California: Stanford University Press, 1962.

———. *Lincoln in Text and Context*. California: Stanford University Press, 1987.

Fehrenbacher, Don E. and Virginia Fehrenbacher. *Recollected Words of Abraham Lincoln*. California: Stanford University Press, 1996.

Foner, Eric. *Reconstruction: America's Unfinished Revolution 1863–1877*. New York: Harper and Row, 1988.

Frank, John P. *Lincoln as a Lawyer*. Chicago: Americana House, 1991.

Gienapp, William. "Abraham Lincoln and Presidential Leadership" in *We Cannot Escape History: Lincoln and the Last Best Hope of Earth,* James McPherson, ed. Urbana, Ill.: University of Illinois Press, 1995.

Guelzo, Allen C. *Abraham Lincoln: Reedemer President*. Grand Rapids: William B. Eerdmans, 1999.

Hattaway, Herman, and Archer Jones. *How the North Won: A Military History of the Civil War*. Urbana, Ill.: University of Illinois Press, 1983.

Hein, David. "The Calvinistic tenor of Abraham Lincoln's religious thought" in *Lincoln Herald*. Harrogate, Tenn.: Lincoln Memorial University Press, vol. 85, no. 4.

Hendrick, Burton J. *Lincoln's War Cabinet*. Boston: Little, Brown, 1946.

Herndon, William H., and Jesse W. Weik. *Herndon's Life of Lincoln*. New York: World Publishing Company, 1943 [reprint of original].

Hertz, Emanuel. *The Hidden Lincoln: From the Letters and Papers of William H. Herndon*. New York: The Viking Press, 1938.

———. *Lincoln Talks*. New York: Viking, 1939.

Holzer, Harold. *The Lincoln-Douglas Debates*. New York: Harper Collins, 1993.

Jaffa, Harry. *Crisis in the House Divided: An Interpretation of the Issues in the Lincoln-Douglas Debates.* Seattle: University of Washington Press, 1959.

Jones, Edgar DeWitt. *Lincoln and the Preachers.* New York: Harper and Brothers, 1948.

Lamon, Ward H. *The Life of Abraham Lincoln: From His Birth to His Inauguration as President.* Boston: James R. Osgood, 1872.

Leidner, Gordon D. "Measuring the Presidents: Modern leadership theory provides a framework for comparing the presidential skills of Lincoln and Davis" in *Columbiad: A Quarterly Review of the War Between the States,* vol. 2, no. 1.

Long, David. *The Jewel of Liberty.* Mechanicsburg, Pa.: Stackpole Books, 1994.

———. "Wartime Democracy: Lincoln and the Midterm Election of 1862," *Columbiad,* vol. 1, no. 1.

McPherson, James. *Abraham Lincoln and the Second American Revolution.* New York: Oxford University Press, 1990.

———. *Battle Cry of Freedom.* Oxford University Press, 1988.

———. *We Cannot Escape History.* Urbana, Ill.: University of Illinois Press, 1995.

———. *Drawn With the Sword.* Oxford University Press, 1996.

Miers, Earl Schenk, ed. *Lincoln Day by Day: A Chronology, 1809–1865.* Washington, D.C.: Lincoln Sesquicentennial Commission, 1960.

Monaghan, Jay. "New Light on the Lincoln-Rutledge Romance," *Abraham Lincoln Quarterly* 3. 1944.

Neely, Mark E. *The Fate of Liberty: Abraham Lincoln and Civil Liberties.* New York: Oxford University Press, 1991.

———. *The Abraham Lincoln Encyclopedia.* New York: Da Capo, 1982.

———. *The Last Best Hope of Earth: Abraham Lincoln and the Promise of America.* Cambridge, Mass.: Harvard University Press, 1993.

Nevins, Allan. *The Emergence of Lincoln.* New York: Charles Scribners Sons, 1950.

Nicolay, John G. and John Hay, eds. *Complete Works of Lincoln.* New York: Francis D. Tandy, 1905.

Oates, Stephen. *With Malice Toward None.* New York: Harper and Row, 1977.

Paludan, Phillip Shaw. *The Presidency of Abraham Lincoln.* Kansas: University Press of Kansas, 1994.

———. "Emancipating the Republic" in *We Cannot Escape History: Lincoln and the Last Best Hope of Earth.* James McPherson, ed. Urbana, Ill.: University of Illinois Press, 1995.

Peterson, Merrill D. *Lincoln in American Memory.* New York: Oxford University Press, 1994.

Pratt, Harry E. *Concerning Mr. Lincoln.* Springfield, Ill.: Abraham Lincoln Association, 1944.

Randall, J. G. *Lincoln the President: Springfield to Gettysburg.* New York: Dodd, Mead, and Company, 1946.

———. *Lincoln the President: Midstream.* New York: Dodd, Mead, and Company, 1952.

Rice, Allen T. *Reminiscences of Abraham Lincoln by Distinguished Men of His Time.* New York: North American Review, 1888.

Riddle, Donald Wayne. *Lincoln Runs for Congress.* Springfield: Abraham Lincoln Association, 1948.

Sandburg, Carl. *Abraham Lincoln: The Prairie Years.* 2 vols. New York: Charles Scribners Sons, Sangamon Edition, 1943.

———. *Abraham Lincoln: The War Years.* 4 vols. New York: Charles Scribners Sons, Sangamon Edition, 1943.

Simon, Paul. *Lincoln's Preparation for Greatness: The Illinois Legislative Years.* Norman, Okla.: University of Oklahoma Press, 1965.

Speed, Joshua. *Reminiscences of Abraham Lincoln and Notes of a Visit to California.* Louisville, Ky.: John P. Morgan and Company, 1884.

Stakelberg, Count S. "Tolstoi Holds Lincoln World's Greatest Hero," *New York World,* 7 February 1901.

Steers, Edward. *His Name is Still Mudd: the Case Against Doctor Samuel Alexander Mudd.* Thomas Publications, 1997.

Strozier, Charles B. *Lincoln's Quest for Union: Public and Private Meanings.* New York: Basic Books, 1982.

Tarbell Papers. Allegheny College. John Hill to Ida M. Tarbell, Columbus, Ga., 4 April 1896; and John Hill to Ida M. Tarbell, Columbus, Ga., 17 February 1896.

Temple, Wayne C. *Abraham Lincoln: From Skeptic to Prophet.* Mahomet, Ill.: Mayhaven, 1995.

Thomas, Benjamin P. "The Individuality of Lincoln," *Bulletin of the Abraham Lincoln Association.* No. 32, September 1933.

———. *Abraham Lincoln.* New York: Alfred Knopf, 1952.

———. *Lincoln's New Salem.* Springfield: Abraham Lincoln Association, 1934.

Trueblood, Elton. *Abraham Lincoln, Theologian of American Anguish.* New York: Harper and Row, 1973.

Ward, Geoffrey C. *The Civil War, an Illustrated History.* New York: Alfred A. Knopf, 1991.

Warren, Louis. *Lincoln's Youth: Indiana Years 1816–1830.* New York: Appleton-Century-Crofts, 1959.

Williams, Thomas H. *Lincoln and the Generals.* New York: Alfred A. Knopf, 1952.

Wills, Gary. *Lincoln at Gettysburg: The Words that Remade America.* New York: Simon and Schuster, 1992.

Wilson, Douglas and Rodney Davis, eds. *Herndon's Informants: Letters, Interviews, and Statements About Abraham Lincoln.* Urbana, Ill.: University of Illinois Press, 1998.

Wilson, Douglas L. *Honor's Voice: The Transformation of Abraham Lincoln.* New York: Alfred A. Knopf, 1998.

Wolf, William J. *The Religion of Abraham Lincoln.* New York: Seabury Press, 1963.

Zall, P. M., ed. *Abe Lincoln Laughing.* Berkely, Calif.: University of California Press, 1982.

Index

142